Praise for *Frederick*

From an American perspective, it's difficult to imagine the enormity of an event like the Rwandan genocide, how it changed and traumatized every single human life. But through Frederick's story, we see how trauma can bloom into triumph when watered with streams of hope. It's a story of transformation that can transform us all.

—TRICIA GOYER
USA TODAY BEST-SELLING AUTHOR
OF OVER 40 BOOKS, BLOGGER, AND
HOMESCHOOLING MOM OF 6

Wow—what a remarkable story! *Frederick* has all the elements that make a great biography: tragedy, persistence, vision, and redemption. Read this one. You'll be the better for it.

—ANDY ANDREWS
NEW YORK TIMES BEST-SELLING
AUTHOR OF HOW DO YOU KILL 11
MILLION PEOPLE?, THE NOTICER,
AND THE TRAVELER'S GIFT

Frederick pulls at your heart from every direction. The trials he endured are unfathomable, yet his faith is unshakable. Amy Parker shares his story so vividly and candidly that the reader feels as if they are in Rwanda—heart pounding, uncertainty and fear choking and paralyzing them—as they not only dive deeper into Frederick's story of obstacles and overcoming, but also into their personal stories, causing readers to look inward, refueled to conquer their own disablements with boundless hope.

—LAURA L. SMITH
AUTHOR AND SPEAKER

In only 10,000 days and counting, Frederick Ndabaramiye has lived through a genocide, lost his hands, found his calling, and eliminated the word *impossible* from his vocabulary. I'd say he's off to an amazing start—and I'd say he has a lot to teach us all.

—ROBERT D. SMITH
AUTHOR OF 20,000 DAYS
AND COUNTING

When you need a dose of can-do spirit, remember Frederick! A powerful story of faith, trust, and overcoming severe obstacles.

—DIANE STORTZ
AUTHOR OF THE WOMAN'S GUIDE
TO READING THE BIBLE IN A YEAR

The drive and innovation of this one young man is astounding. Through Frederick's story, you'll get a powerful look at the potential of the human spirit and a true representation of the resilience of the Rwandan people. And in the end, you'll no doubt be inspired to put that potential and resilience to work tackling social problems around the world.

—BRETT SMITH, PhD
FOUNDING DIRECTOR, CENTER
FOR SOCIAL ENTREPRENEURSHIP
AT MIAMI UNIVERSITY

frederick

frederick

A Story of

Boundless Hope

FREDERICK NDABARAMIYE
and AMY PARKER

W Publishing Group

AN IMPRINT OF THOMAS NELSON

Published in Nashville, Tennessee, by W Publishing, an imprint of Thomas Nelson.

Author represented exclusively by Bill Reeves at WTA Services, LLC, Smyrna, Tennessee.

Thomas Nelson titles may be purchased in bulk for educational, business, fund-raising, or sales promotional use. For information, please e-mail SpecialMarkets@ThomasNelson.com.

Library of Congress Control Number: 2014942536

ISBN-13: 9780529101198
ISBN-13: 9780718031404(ITPE)

Printed in the United States of America

14 15 16 17 18 19 RRD 6 5 4 3 2 1

This book is dedicated to my mother and Madame Carr. Your faith and support have carried me through. And to the people of Rwanda, I hope that my healing will become a part of your own.

Lord, *I have called daily upon You;*
I have stretched out my hands to You.
Will You work wonders for the dead?
Shall the dead arise and praise You?
Shall Your lovingkindness be declared in the grave?
Or Your faithfulness in the place of destruction?

—Psalm 88:9–11 nkjv

contents

contents

foreword

When I first met Frederick, he was still just a kid at
the Imbabazi Orphanage in Rwanda. I was immediately awe-
struck by the beaming smile of this young man who had been
through so much, who had lost his hands to a group of ruthless
murderers. I wondered how a kid could have suffered so much
and yet still be smiling, still be filled with such a contagious
hope.

And then the other question hit: *How in the world is he sitting
there painting a landscape with no hands?!*

During his first trip to the United States, I watched him
adapt quickly to a world that, before stepping off that plane, he
had never even fathomed—a world with car washes, five-lane
roads, and a set of prosthetic hands just for him. He blew us all
away with his abilities. And he's been doing it ever since.

When he headed back to Rwanda with those new hands, I
thought, *Our work is done here; Frederick's story has a happy ending.* But then when I went back to see him in Rwanda, there he was

teaching a group of disabled people how to play volleyball—with *no hands*. So we did a little filming and closed that storybook with another unbelievable happy ending. *But then I went back again,* and there he was in a two-room building teaching the disabled and beggars how to paint and speak English.

That moment was a turning point for me. That's when this kid truly took hold of my heart. That's when I learned to never underestimate Frederick Ndabaramiye; that no matter what he's doing, he's only getting started.

Over the years, Frederick and I have grown to be good friends. I see him at least once a year now, at the Rwandan Fête in Columbus or at his home in Rwanda. But no matter how often I see him, one thing never changes: my absolute astonishment at his abilities.

Whatever you throw at him, he'll catch it. And he'll do so with a smile.

A few years ago, Pastor Tom Mullins invited Frederick to speak at Christ Fellowship Church in Palm Beach Gardens, Florida. It's a huge church with about forty thousand attendees over the course of a weekend, including several big celebrities, and Frederick spoke at their services. As that young man delivered his story to the church, the entire congregation was completely mesmerized. No one moved. No one coughed. No one shuffled in their seats. You could have heard a pin drop. Afterward, Pastor Mullins came to me and said, "Jack, I started this church twenty years ago, and I've never had this kind of response from anyone who's been here."

At the Columbus Zoo, we've adopted a mission and a method

to "touch the heart to teach the mind." We know that to initiate change and generate awareness as advocates for the animal kingdom, we have to begin by touching the hearts of humans. Frederick, unknowingly, takes this same approach, and in doing so, has initiated great change in his town in Rwanda and quite literally around the world.

The Lord has to be with him for him to do all that he does.

When he came to Hanger Prosthetics to get his new fingers, they were all baffled by his ability to instantly put the prosthetics to work. And do you know the first thing he told them he wanted to use the fingers for? To build himself a house, of course. The entire team just sat in awe watching this young man as he operated those fingers with the agility and skill it takes most people months and years to learn.

I've tried myself to see how long I could go without my hands, trying to do what Frederick does day in and day out. I tried to get dressed, brush my teeth, and fasten my belt without the help of my hands. And I'll tell you, after about thirty minutes, I gave up.

One time, while Frederick was staying with my wife, Suzi, and me, I was loading the car with suitcases when I heard Sue scream, "Stop, Frederick! Get off!" I looked up to see him riding down the road on my bicycle. He had seen it in the garage and decided to go for a ride. We hadn't even noticed, and he was doing just fine, riding it as well as she or I would. But it scared Suzi to see him riding off down the road, steering a bicycle with no hands; she and I had never seen anything so incredible.

Another time, he was staying with us in Columbus, and we were getting ready to go to an event. We were running a little late, and he came out and asked Suzi, "Will you help me button these last two buttons?"

I just looked at him, my mouth hung open, and I finally asked, "Well, how the heck did you get the other four buttoned?!"

Frederick just laughed that big laugh, as he always does, like a magician who never tells his tricks.

So let me tell you, whatever this magician has up his sleeve, you want to see it. Whatever he has to say, you want to hear it. Whatever you can learn from his life, you don't ever want to forget it.

Because of Frederick, I look at life differently. I thank God for my health and the things I can do. And I ask Him to help me be more like Frederick and face the things I *think* I can't do.

When I get discouraged, I tell myself, *If Frederick can do this, I can too.*

Frederick has shown me—as he's shown everyone privileged to know him—that everything is possible if you have a little faith.

Today, you become one of the privileged.

Today, you meet Frederick.

—JACK HANNA
DIRECTOR EMERITUS OF THE COLUMBUS ZOO
HOST OF *JACK HANNA'S INTO THE WILD* AND
JACK HANNA'S WILD COUNTDOWN

prologue

Countless historical and political accounts have been written about the Rwandan genocide. This is not one of them. I observed as a child, watching with confusion and defenseless acceptance as merciless killings swept through my country, my neighborhood, my family.

I am simply a Rwandan—one of millions with harrowing stories to tell. More than that, I am a survivor, one whose tragedy has propelled me into a man I could have never been otherwise. Whatever the circumstances, I believe—I know—survival makes us stronger. Survival makes us smarter. Survival provides a unique fuel for our passion for life.

I was only eleven when the genocide earthquaked my foundations of security and hope. The event and its aftershocks would leave me forever changed—mentally, spiritually, emotionally, and perhaps most obviously, physically. Yet, in a strange way, in those mysterious ways known only by our God, those perpetrators of the genocide would leave me with an iron will and an undeniable purpose.

But in order to gain those gifts, I would first have to journey to the brink of death and back again . . . and again. My adherence to my faith would cost me my hands. But just as my faith drove me to my troubles, my faith would lead me out again. And on the other side, I would realize a clearer, bolder picture of who God wanted me to be, while being newly equipped with the passion, hope, and faith needed to paint that picture.

It was only after losing my hands that I was finally able to grasp God's purpose for my life: to strip the world of its excuses and replace them with hope and inspiration to fulfill the dreams God has placed in the hearts of His people.

In Rwanda, we've begun that work of rebuilding hope in very tangible ways, but I know there's more.

I know this story isn't just for me. It isn't just for Rwanda. I know this story is for everyone. Because I now know that in the end, we are all broken. And we are all searching for hope.

If your eyes have been darkened by hate or guilt or despair . . . if forgiveness is a faraway, unnavigable utopia . . . if you're seeking hope where hopelessness abounds . . . I have a story for you.

It's a story with unfathomable depths of grief and insurmountable heights of hope. But it's a true story. It's my story. And I hope that, in some small way, it can be a turning point for your own.

one

new beginnings

"*If you feel that the world is sometimes a cold place,
that the human spirit cannot beat back despair, think of
Frederick Ndabaramiye. . . . Think of him, and smile.*"
—CHARLIE GIBSON

"You ready?"

The guy spoke to me as he adjusted the height on his tripod. I had never seen a camera so big. Another person was pulling a chair a few centimeters to the left. Someone else repositioned the traditional African mask—the only object relatively familiar to me—that sat in Charlene's living room. A light as bright as the African sun shined on the man across from me.

Did he say his name was Charlie?

"Frederick." Charlene kneeled down in front of me. "Are you okay? Are you ready to start?"

I had a basic understanding of English, but my ability to speak the language was much less developed. Even so, I knew the answer to both of her questions: no and no.

A few weeks ago, I had boarded a huge, mysterious vehicle I

had never seen before and trusted it to carry me—through the air—to the other side of the world, to a place I knew very little about. I was overwhelmed before I even boarded the airplane. I had never been to Kigali, Rwanda's capital city where we would be flying out from, but even at nighttime, I could tell that it was larger than any town I'd ever seen. As we drove to the airport, an infinite field of lights rose up all around me. I could only imagine how big it looked in the daytime.

The airport was monstrously large and full of people, a lot of them speaking English and other languages I didn't understand. Upstairs in the terminal, glass cases held cigars and candies and liquors and sodas in endless varieties. Stern-faced, uniformed men behind glass walls asked me all kinds of questions about where I was going and what I was doing there. They peered at my passport before waving me through to go meet my fate on that big white plane.

"How long will it take to get there?" I asked Tony, my translator, at least a hundred times. He would answer and pull out a map to show me where we were now and where we were going, but it did little to calm my anxiety.

"Have you ever been inside an airplane before?"

"Yes." He smiled at me, anticipating my next question.

"What does it look like?"

He described rows of seats and windows with a driver in the front, something that sounded like a really, really big bus. Except for the part where it flew in the air. I couldn't quite wrap my mind around the image, though, until we climbed aboard. Tony found our seats and let me slide in first, by the window, where I could see that the ground was already several meters below us.

I didn't sleep all night. I stared out that window the entire time, watching the ground as it fell out from under us while an intense pressure pushed me back in my seat. And I didn't stop watching until the ground rose back up to hold the plane so that I could step out onto solid ground.

After a whole night and day of travel, I exited the airplane through a long tunnel. At the end of that tunnel, I discovered a dizzying world beyond anything I'd ever imagined, even after all the stories I had heard about America. There were lights, so many lights, and voices yelling over loudspeakers in words I didn't understand. There were a thousand white people; I had never seen so many before. Even though I knew they wouldn't really use my head as alligator bait, as I had been warned as a child, I was still fearful at the sight of them.

How would I speak to them? Would they even care what I had to say?

"I'll be right here to help you, the whole time," Tony reassured me, sensing my increased anxiety.

After we picked up our bags, we made our way to the exit to find a car. Standing there was a lady holding up a sign that said, "Frederick." When she saw me, she starting waving and calling, "Frederick! Frederick!" I knew a handful of people from the United States, but she wasn't one of them.

I walked closer and asked her, "How do you know me?"

"Charlene Jendry gave me a picture of you," she explained. "My name is Margaret. I'm going to be your driver." She grinned.

I had never seen a lady drive a car before. In Rwanda today, you sometimes see women driving, but back then, it seemed so strange to me. However, this trip had already been an adventure of many firsts, so I followed her to the car.

As we loaded our luggage into Margaret's car, Tony announced, "Now we're getting close."

We drove away from all of the people in the airport terminal only to see just as many cars on the wide, flat road. There was row after row of very tall houses. No one at all was walking on the roads until we got to a smaller road, but even then, there were only a few people running and riding bicycles. No one was carrying goods on their heads to or from the market. I saw no burlap bags of charcoal, no baskets of avocados or bananas. Yet everyone seemed to be in a focused hurry to go *somewhere*.

I had a hard time falling asleep that night, my first night in America. That was probably due, in part, to the television being on all night. I sat there in a dizzied daze watching the flickering images of white people talking and dancing and leisurely reading books. I tried to translate the fast, fluent conversations, and I swayed and danced to the music. It was all so surreal.

I was in America.

After I had settled into Charlene's house—which felt more like a hotel—I tried to follow all of the advice and tips I had been given about travel to this new world, even down to the food. Back at the orphanage, a lady from Canada had visited and told me that Americans ate a lot of fast food, that they had hamburgers and hot dogs everywhere. However, when we went to one restaurant, a place where a guy in a tall white hat chopped and cooked our food on the sizzling table in front of us, I tried to order a hamburger, and I was promptly told that they didn't even have it on the menu. But I was quite pleased to discover that they had rice and mixed vegetables instead. To top it off, the guy even made a volcano out of onions with real smoke coming out of it! That place helped to make me feel a bit more at home.

When I finally did get to try a hamburger, I decided then that I would just stick to the rice and vegetables. But I discovered I really liked the french fries. And chicken. Chicken was my favorite.

Toward the end of my stay in the U.S., I was also able to go visit my friend David Jiranek in New York. David was a photographer whom I'd met at the Imbabazi Orphanage in Rwanda. When he heard that I was coming to the States, he arranged for me to come to his house and meet his family.

New York City was huge, much bigger than Kigali. There were people everywhere—on foot and in cars. And there were the tallest houses, taller than anything I had ever imagined.

One day while I was there, David and his wife, Cricket, took me to see a parade. I had never seen anything like it before. There were so many people—even more than before—crowded into the streets. But the oddest thing of all were these big, colorful plastic people floating in the air. They had ropes tied to them that ran down to men and women standing on the ground, guiding the floating people down the street.

David, Cricket, and I were watching the parade when I became mesmerized by one of the tall houses. I just stood there, looking up, trying to see the top, thinking about the people inside and imagining what they were doing, what their houses looked like from the inside. After a few moments, I looked back to David, but he was gone. I spun around. Cricket was gone too. No one looked familiar, and I had absolutely no idea where I was. I didn't have a phone number or an address—nothing. I walked quickly through the streets, watching in all directions, trying to remember what color everyone was wearing. Then, from out of nowhere, I heard someone calling my name, "Frederick!" I turned, and there stood Cricket. I was never so relieved to see a familiar face. From then on, I insisted that I stand in the middle of the group, and I never fell behind again.

The food in New York was unbelievable. Every time I ordered a meal, they brought me enough for five people. And then they kept asking me if I wanted *more*. A guy in one restaurant came by and asked me if I wanted more iced tea.

"*Oya*," I answered, which means "no" in Rwanda.

But he brought me more tea anyway.

At the end of the meal, when he had a moment, I asked him playfully, "So why did you bring me more tea when I said I didn't want any?"

Confused, he answered, "But you said yes."

"I said, '*Oya*.' That means 'no' back home in Rwanda."

He laughed. "Well, in America, 'oh yeah,' means yes!"

I had no idea! After that, I just learned to say, "No, thank you."

I experienced so many new things during that trip to New York. The first time I stepped inside a train, I didn't know what was going to happen. I felt like I was about to fly, but then the train took off, I lost my balance, and people all around me scrambled to catch me. At the next stop, I found a seat and sat down from then on. I thought it was so funny to sit inside while watching the people whirring by outside.

After lunch one day, I experienced the sweet, cold taste of ice cream for the first time. We didn't have ice cream in Rwanda, but after trying it in New York, I was always hungry for it—no matter how much I had eaten.

David also took me out on the ocean in a boat; that was the first time in my life to even touch a boat. I felt like we were going so fast out on the huge, wavy water. It was scary and thrilling at the same time.

Even with all the sights and sounds of the big city, the most amazing thing about my trip was right there at home, near Charlene's house, at the Columbus Zoo. Some may think that because I'm from Africa, there are lions roaming in my backyard. But in the volcanic mountain ranges of Rwanda, gorillas are one of the few exotic animals that make their home there. And I had never even been to see those. Although I had seen photos of the lions and hippos on the other side of our country in Akagera National Park, it seemed that only wealthy Rwandans and international tourists were privy to viewing the animals that roamed the park. There, at the Columbus Zoo, every animal you could think of—gorillas, elephants, rhinos, and then some—was right there in front of you, nestled into their own little piece of Africa or Australia or wherever they were from.

Even if someone had told me about all of these things before I arrived, I never could have imagined it. Never would it have prepared me for the experience of actually being there—the completely new smells, the change in the weather, the size and shapes of the trees, the different hue of the sky.

And I never would have dreamed that a group of people a world away would care about a young Rwandan man with no hands, that all of this was taking place because some compassionate people here in the United States wanted to make sure that I received my new fingers.

These guys with the cameras had been following me around Columbus to document the whole thing, so I had grown used to them. Yet now they wanted to film me talking to the guy sitting across from me: Charlie Gibson, that was his name. He seemed really nice, so I wasn't really worried about that. And I had a translator, so I knew we would be able to communicate. Still, I couldn't shake the feeling that what I was about to do would change my life in ways I could never fathom. I knew that talking about what had happened to me would force me to remember everything, to feel the pain all over again, to watch those people die, to remember the men who watched and laughed as they cut off my hands.

Yet there was a propelling peace inside of me, a part of me that knew, without a doubt, that this was exactly what I was supposed to be doing. Although all evidence pointed to the contrary, I was assured that right here in this living room was exactly where I belonged.

For now.

An unbelievable future waited ahead of me. But first, I would have to tell the world about my past, about how I came to be a young Rwandan man with no hands.

Charlene watched protectively as the guy finished with the light and came to clip a tiny microphone onto my shirt.

She spoke softly. "Frederick, are you ready?"

I looked her in the eyes, collected my voice, and said, "Yes."

two

killing a country

"After being there in 1982, Rwanda was the last country I'd expect a genocide to happen in."
—JACK HANNA

When I lost my hands, everyone thought the genocide was over.

And maybe, to the outside world, it was. But here in Rwanda, the heart of Africa, the fear of sweeping, imminent death was still very much alive.

It had never really gone away.

———✕——✕———

For me, the genocide began with the blaring of a loudspeaker outside my sister's house. After school had dismissed in March, I made the five-hour walk from Ramba to Gishwati to stay with my older sister Beatrice and her husband. I had planned to spend the break helping my sister with chores and my brother-in-law with the shop they had in town, but I would soon learn that I'd be returning home much sooner than expected.

I was ten or eleven at the time. I'm not sure exactly how old—then or now. It seems in Western countries, everyone knows their birth time to the *minute*. I don't know my birth time to the *year*. It's not that birthdays aren't important—they are—we just don't focus on the day. Or, I guess, even the year. We consider all of life a miracle, especially now, in a country so well known for its deaths.

This particular day, however, would be a day I would always remember. This day would later be lamented by presidents, recorded in history books, dissected through debates, and memorialized in museums. Countless press conferences and articles and books would try to explain what happened that day, try to define the aftermath that followed, try to answer the questions that weighed heavy on the hearts of all who watched the terrors unfold, either in person or eventually on a television screen.

Why was the president's plane shot down? How did the Hutus come to believe that killing their own president was the best for the country? When did this country become so embedded with hate, and what made it fester into a full-blown epidemic that would decimate a nation? How would a country ever recover from such a devastating blow to its economy, to its infrastructure, to its population?

Most of the outside world had few answers to these questions. Even for those of us inside the country, we had seen the signs, we knew the history, but never would we have predicted such an outcome.

It couldn't be disputed, however, that Rwanda's political past was littered with horrific atrocities fueled mostly by racism. There had been three races, or tribes, that made up most of the Rwandan population: the majority Hutus, a word meaning "cultivators" or "planters"; the elite Tutsis, a traditionally taller, more slender people, with their roots firmly planted in royalty; and the Twas, a people very short in stature, very few in number, but very big in mystery and magic. The Twas, because of their small number and secretive nature, were rarely seen; they kept to themselves.

Throughout the last several decades, there had been continuous tension between the two larger people groups. The Hutus vastly outnumbered the Tutsis; however the Tutsis ruled over the Hutus because of their royal status. Then, when the king died in 1959, the Hutus rose up to overthrow the Tutsi monarchy, killing many Tutsis in the process. It seems there were external forces at work too, as Rwanda was officially under Belgian rule, but even after Rwanda was declared independent in 1962, the uprisings continued. The Tutsis would attempt a retaliation, but being largely outnumbered, it was their tribe that repeatedly received the bulk of the collateral damage.

In 1973, the Hutus finally secured their rule when they overthrew the Tutsi government and Juvénal Habyarimana became president. This seemed to calm much of the fighting for a period, although propaganda and discrimination still fueled hatred against the Tutsis.

Meanwhile, over time, the two tribes had blended, leaving few physical characteristics that separated the "races." Still, the government was issuing its citizens the identity cards that were very clearly marked "Hutu" and "Tutsi." My parents' cards, for instance, said "Hutu." But for most of us, high in the hills, in small villages and towns, it didn't much matter to us what our neighbor's identity card said. For the Hutus in power, however, it would later become an indicator of who would live and who would die.

Although a Hutu president was in office, it seemed the radical Hutu groups were still not satisfied. And soon these Hutus and their supporters would launch a plan in hopes of wiping out the Tutsis once and for all.

For me, that day would obliterate everything I knew about safety, peace, forgiveness, and love. And in ways that only God can explain, it would make me a better man.

It was April 7, 1994.

Around five o'clock that morning, Beatrice called for me. "*Byuka*, Frederick!" Wake up! "*Ujye kuvoma.*" It was time to get the water.

My sister's early wake-up call was nothing new. But the loudspeaker was. The box shouted at me from a nearby mud-bricked wall. The staticky, robotic voice told me that my president was dead. His plane had crashed, and the voice blamed the crash on my Tutsi neighbors. It ordered me to stay home and told me that I was in danger if I didn't.

It was then that I realized just how far I was from my mother's arms and my father's laugh. And even though I was nearly a man, I wished I were there, back in the safety of home.

"*Ujye kuvoma!*" My sister's voice soothed and startled me at once. "Go get the water!"

No matter what that box threatened, having no water was an

even greater threat. This time of year, watering the potatoes was vital. The heavy rains of April would often bring disease, and we had to treat the potatoes with a mixture of medicine and water. But more than that, the crops, the meals, the washbasins—*everything* revolved around the water. As the village formed, a pond had been dug in the center, down below, to collect rain for the families who lived there. The wealthy people would keep their cows there, and the rest of us would walk down to get water for cooking, bathing, washing clothes, and watering the crops.

That morning, just like every morning, I hoisted an empty jerrican onto my head and walked the dirt path, smoothed by thousands of feet before me, that led to water. Looking back now, I realize that jug had to be as big as I was, but I thought nothing of it then. Gathering water was simply a child's job. Some of the other kids would collect wood or even tend to the cows—the entire wealth of a family depended on those cows. Regardless, we all pitched in; there was always a way to help.

My water journey began in the dark of the morning, but as soon as the light from the rising sun struck the mist hanging from the lush green canopy, it became a forest of diamonds. Sometimes a colobus monkey or two would flit down to greet me, chastising me for trespassing, chasing each other and squabbling like children. That was the toughest part of the job: trying not to lose my balance from laughing so hard.

Following the path down, I'd walk past the homes, through the canopy of trees, beyond the fields of potatoes and maize, by the *ibikuyu* (the shelters where the cows slept and ate), and wade into the cacophony of cows to gather water. The trip back up was a little more precarious, climbing with a much heavier jug on my head. The entire trip only took about an hour, but when I returned, I knew they'd be waiting on me.

As I neared my sister's home, I saw her outside, looking across the road. Together we watched as a group approached the roadblock that had just been set up. "Put down your water!" the men ordered. It was obvious, even to a boy (or *especially* to a boy), that these men were not from our military. Instead of uniforms, they wore shirts with brightly colored patterns. Their glazed eyes held us with crazed stares. But perhaps most notable were the *imipanga*, or machetes, that hung by their sides.

As the men searched the people, one announced, "We've found *inyenzi!*"

Inyenzi. "Cockroaches." It's no doubt a word now emblazoned in the minds of Tutsis, of all Rwandans. For years, Hutus had been taught to believe that Tutsis were inhuman, cockroaches or monkeys hiding their tails in their pants. Some people actually believed it. Blasting from the loudspeakers, on the radios, in the roadblocks, that one word would be wielded as a weapon against the Tutsi people throughout the genocide and beyond. For me, even as a young Hutu, I quickly learned that when I heard the word, I had to run.

Before that spring day in 1994, the Hutus and Tutsis in my village seemed to live in harmony—for as long as I could remember, anyway. We were neighbors, friends, living side by side all throughout Rwanda. Unless you were to ask for our identity cards, you probably couldn't tell the difference between the two tribes.

But that all changed drastically when the plane crashed late in the night of April 6. What I didn't know—what most Rwandans didn't know—is that the crash was the catalyst, the signal, that moved the killers into action. The attack had been planned, weapons had been stockpiled, and the killers laid low, waiting for this event to set it all in motion. By blaming the death of the Hutu president on the Tutsis, the demented hope was that the decades-long resentment toward the Tutsis would combust into an all-out wildfire, swiftly clearing the land of the privileged minority. A Tutsi ID card, a tall, thin physique, or just an elongated nose—any of these could become a death sentence for our neighbors and friends. Even sympathizing with the Tutsis, as many Hutus soon discovered, would be a final and fatal act of compassion.

My first encounter with this was there, outside my sister's home, helplessly watching the scene at the roadblock unfold. After three girls in the crowd obediently placed their water jugs on the ground, the men with *imipanga*—who would come to be infamously known as the *Interahamwe*—began to beat them. Simply because they were suspected Tutsis. It seemed unbelievably heinous at the time, but over the days and weeks and months to come, this would be one of the most merciful encounters with the Interahamwe.

As the men beat the girls, another voice rang out. *"Kurorera!"* "Stop that!" It was Hamatha, a well-known blind man, a villager who owned a company making rugs. Seeing him, the men stopped, and Hamatha pulled the girls into the safety of his arms.

Beatrice had seen enough. She turned to me and said, "You have to go back home." So with shaky hands and an unsettled stomach, I ate one last breakfast with my sister, and we made plans for my return.

The following day, I shouldered my belongings and a ten-kilogram burlap bag of potatoes and waved good-bye to my sister and her husband. The world had changed since I had taken that same path two weeks ago. Death waited behind every tree, beyond every bush. Each leaded step felt as if I were taking my last. I knew those men with machetes were going to kill me.

And then, there they were.

"Where are you coming from?" one demanded. "Who are you? Tell us the names of five people you know!"

At that moment, I could barely remember my own name, much less five others. Then my sister's face, waving good-bye, flashed into memory, and her husband, and somehow the names of three others. With a merciful, arrogant wave of a club, I escaped death—without even a beating—and continued the long walk home.

While the walk from Gishwati to Ramba only takes about five hours, it felt like years. When I finally looked up and saw that maize-colored house on the hill, when I smelled the pungent smoke rising from my mother's fire, when I saw my father's grin, I was enveloped in the relief of home.

A few days later, I made the four-hour trip to the international market in Kabaya to buy goods that we didn't have in Ramba. As subdued as it was, the Kabaya market was bustling compared to the quiet village back home. The market tables were laden with the day's harvest: crisp green beans, potatoes, peanuts, carrots, and cassava. Basket-topped villagers gathered food for their families. Used clothing from the rich countries, like America and the UK, flapped like flags in the breeze. I felt like a rich man myself, loaded down with potatoes, avocados, bananas, and meats. And I could already taste the sugar-cane snack I would have on the long trip home.

Pushing through the crowd, I rounded a corner and came to an immediate halt. There stood three men, two with guns and a big guy with a club. The big guy, with his other hand, pulled a knife up to my heart and looked at the others. "I'd say he looks like one of those Tutsi cockroaches. What do you say, brothers?"

Six void eyes, set deep above three stony smiles, seemed to look right through me. The big guy pushed the knife into my skin until blood escaped around the point. Warmth ran down my chest, but I didn't look down.

I couldn't move. I couldn't speak. I closed my eyes.

"Don't kill him!"

I heard the words, and the knife jumped. Or maybe I did.

"He's my son. I love him."

I knew the voice wasn't my father's, but I recognized it just the same. It was Hamatha, the blind man. I had no idea why or how he was at the Kabaya market that day. But I did know one thing: the same man who had saved the girls outside my sister's house would save my life as well.

Although temporarily saved, I wouldn't feel safe again. Not for a very long time. And when I arrived home, it seemed the terror had spread to epidemic proportions.

Men were streaming through the village announcing, "Go, go! The country is being taken over! If you stay, you die!"

Within a matter of days, our president had died, our Tutsi neighbors were being propagated as our enemies, and the Interahamwe had already killed tens of thousands. So when men came to our village claiming to be the military, telling our families to leave or die, we needed little convincing. Our village gathered and decided: the next day we would seek refuge across the border, in Zaire (now the Democratic Republic of the Congo).

An eerie quiet filled the village that night. We built a fire, we cooked, we packed, and we prepared to leave on another search for safety.

The following afternoon, my father gathered our family and all the food and supplies we could carry. My mother, a rolled woven mat balanced on her head, stoically walked ahead of me. I pulled our sheep behind me.

As the village gathered and our group grew larger, the adults agreed it was best to keep the children on the inside of the group with the adults surrounding them. There had been whispers of Interahamwe fleeing Rwanda, dressed as villagers, walking among us. So the adults formed a protective circle around us. And that's how we walked, for three days, toward the setting sun.

During those three days, it felt as if those sheep and I walked Rwanda's thousand hills a thousand times. There was no time. Day and night, we trudged the small footpaths up and down the winding hills, through the muddy rains. The sheep would drag and pull, and I'd fall behind.

"Run!" my sister would call from ahead, but it took all of my might and mind to shove one blistered foot ahead of the other. Yet when guns or bombs would shatter the silence, we all mustered the strength to scurry a little higher, a little farther.

Then, through the mist, I caught a glimpse of the volcano's red glow hovering in the night sky. We were close.

But as the African sun warmed and the winds stirred, we were blasted with the sweet, musty stench of rot and began to wonder if we had escaped anything at all. Our promised land, Mugunga, turned out to be a refugee camp with no food, no room, and no medical care—only a hopeless sea of diseased and dying people.

Fighting often broke out within the camp because even the most basic necessities were scarce compared to the enormity of need. There was no water readily available, and the walk to water was too far for children to carry the full jerricans back to the camp. To retrieve water, a strong adult would have to walk an *ibicugutu*, a type of wooden bicycle, for miles down to Lake Kivu and balance the jugs of water on the bike all the way back. Even then, those five liters of water didn't go very far among thousands of people. Some groups pooled what little money they had and sent someone to the closest village to buy water, but even that option quickly ran dry. Dehydration, exacerbated by the stomach viruses spreading rampantly throughout the packed crowds, quickly took its toll on the masses. Everywhere we looked, people lay on the ground, the African sun sapping them of their last bit of vitality.

There were no buildings around, and relief agencies hadn't yet arrived with tents and supplies. During the day, hoards of people tried to huddle under the few shade trees within the area. The nights were uncomfortably cold, and there was no firewood for warmth or for cooking. Some began cutting down trees, much to the protest of others, to prepare meals. Throughout the camp, explosive brawls broke out as desperate people literally fought for their lives.

Many who didn't fall victim to disease and dehydration got swept along in the current of chaos. One boy from our village, Musa, was connected to his mother by a string. She was caring for her baby when someone walked between them, breaking the string and separating Musa from his mother. He was swallowed in the swirling crowd and never saw his mother again.

As relief agencies arrived, they were overwhelmed with the need. They began organizing people to move out to other camps, and they attempted to reunite lost children with their families. But as people began to fall to dehydration and disease, it wasn't possible to neglect the bodies amassing throughout the camp.

My family was engulfed in the suffering and sadness. Death. Disease. Hunger. Thirst. Indescribable filth. Adults were crying because they had lost their children; children were crying because they lost their parents. The stench of rot and waste was unbearable. Everywhere we looked, hopeless eyes pleaded for help. And we knew that, at any moment, the next person to fall could be one of us.

None of us wanted to admit it.

Finally, it was my big sister, Mukamana, who said it. "Let's go back home. It would be better to die in Rwanda."

And as simply as that, the journey began again.

My father took us a different route home; it would be longer but safer, he reasoned. But I knew it was all in vain. My father, mother, siblings, and these stupid sheep—we were all on a wild goose chase, a futile fight for safety, for peace, for the life that went up in flames in that airplane crash.

Still, stubbornly, ignorantly, hopefully, we journeyed on.

We startled when we saw them at first—stern, heavily armed men in military attire. But then, one nodded his head at me.

"Welcome home."

three

it isn't over

> "Scholars of these sorts of events say that the killers, armed mostly with machetes and clubs, nonetheless did their work five times as fast as the mechanized gas chambers used by the Nazis."
> —PRESIDENT BILL CLINTON

Despite the soldier's welcome, "home" didn't look much like home at all. The lush, green hills of Rwanda were now littered with debris and death. The paths traveled by refugees were strewn with belongings that could be carried no longer, cows that had given up the fight, and most jarring of all, piles of people discarded by the Interahamwe with the sentiment of dirty old rags. Death and fear hung dark and heavy, shrouding my childhood home in a dismal reality: home would never be the same again.

Still, we walked, heading toward whatever home we had left, passing through sights and smells beyond my most gruesome nightmares. My father never seemed to slow or look down, and my mother followed suit, both looking straight ahead as if they could already see our little mud-brick house miles away behind the hills.

But it was hard for a young boy to ignore the decaying bodies—men with missing limbs, exposed women, mutilated children—their screaming faces set in stone by the horrific trauma that had brought them to their demise. The only beneficiaries were once-domesticated dogs turned ravenous by abandonment, now growing fat from the buffet left by the aftermath, a tsunami of evil strengthening and spreading across our tiny country.

We walked through wave after wave of scenes and stenches no child should ever experience, no human being should ever witness. But for me, my family, my fellow Rwandans, this was our new reality. Hope, beauty, innocence, security—these were all unattainable luxuries, luxuries that were no longer a part of our world, stolen from us by our own people.

I stiffened as we approached another roadblock, but then I noticed: these were not the same men. The men were armed, but not with bloody machetes. They wore full military uniforms and stern but compassionate eyes. We didn't feel threatened by them; we didn't feel comforted by them either. The men stopped us, asked my parents a few questions, and let us carry on.

Or something carried us. It couldn't have been hope. No hope could stand against the incessant, insurmountable waves of destruction still pounding the hills of Rwanda. Was it faith? Obstinacy? Or simply an involuntary, instinctual will to live? Whatever it was, it saved us. It carried us through.

When we made it back to the village, it was a village no more. The structures still stood, but like the few people left to inhabit them, they were mere shells of what used to be. The sounds—the shrill laughter of my friends, the locomotive rhythm of mothers washing clothes, the threadbare pants and shirts hanging on the lines, the smell of bananas boiling, even the masses of padding bare feet—they were all gone.

There had been more than three hundred people in our village before April 7. Now, the seven people who were left came out to welcome our weary family of five. They eyed our swollen feet and asked how the camp had been. My mother just shook her head in reply. We all exchanged empty hugs and dry tears, then settled back in to home.

The days that followed were only eerily reminiscent of our life before the crash. We had left most of our possessions behind in the refugee camp. Of course, my immovable mother saw to it that the thin, handwoven mat rolled upon her head had returned with us. The mat had been in our family for years, covering the dirt floors to make our house a home and spread on the grass outside to welcome our guest. My mother saw to it that this piece of our lives survived.

The market was closed for months. We ate mostly bananas during the day and cooked at night so that no one would see the smoke. We were warned to always travel in pairs or groups—as if anyone needed to be warned. We rarely saw other people, mostly dogs and other scavenging animals and birds. Every hand we shook, every person we met was with suspicion. My heart would stop with every creak or bump or coo in the night. The rising sun brought no relief; we were even more wary of what each new day would hold.

We still hadn't heard from my older sister, Valerie. She lived with her husband and three children several hours away. We barely survived the trip to the refugee camp; traveling to check on them was unthinkable. And if we did, who's to say that they would still be there—and not fleeing to a neighboring village or refugee camp or *worse*—when we arrived? We were able to get some news from the radio, and often other villagers or passersby would know who was still missing and who had been killed in each area.

Then, one day, the news arrived: Valerie's family had become yet another Hutu casualty in this senseless genocide declared against the Tutsis. In reality, it was a war that was destroying us all. No one shared any details about their deaths—at least not with me—but we had seen enough to imagine how they had died, how *she* had died. Our only hope and solace was that death had come quickly to them all. After that day, my parents didn't really talk about it again; they didn't have to.

Besides, we had plenty to worry about at home.

The Interahamwe's widespread, calculated execution of hundreds of thousands of Tutsis had rebounded into a mass of chaotic revenge killings. Hutus were killing Tutsis. Tutsis were killing Hutus for killing their families. Hutus were killing Hutus for sympathizing with Tutsis. A crazed evil had gripped our country, and for those of us still here, it almost seemed as if those who had left this world—by whatever means—were the lucky ones.

Yet after months of heart-crushing news—lists of loved ones we'd never see again, houses burned, children missing—reports began to reach our village of a heroic force camping in the mountains and coming down at night to rescue survivors. At first it seemed impossible that anything could stop the evil that had invaded our country. But up from the ashes rose a band of Tutsi rebels, the Rwandese Patriotic Front (RPF). And slowly and deliberately, the RPF exhibited to the world its ability to do what no one else had dared: end the killing spree that had taken the lives of one million Rwandan citizens. In July 1994, the RPF captured the capital city of Kigali, overpowering the Interahamwe and sending the Hutu government scattering. This is the event historically known as the end of the genocide.

On the opposite side of the country from Kigali, we were able to leave our village for the first time in months. At the time I didn't really know that the genocide had ended, or even that this horror had been donned with the name *genocide*, but I knew that it felt like the beginning of hope. For those living in Rwanda, the end had been gradual, spreading throughout the country as the RPF pushed out the killers like a tide rolling out to sea. But unlike the tide, no one dared to predict if or when it would rise again.

Four years after the killing spree, the Interahamwe were no longer seen in our country. They were rumored to be hiding out in the Congo where they had first fled, hidden among the Tutsi families who thought they had escaped them. In December 1995, the first suspects were officially named and charged with acts of genocide. And just as Rwandans had been the ones to end the genocide, Rwandans would act as jury and judge for many of the genocidaires. Taking care of our own, I would come to learn, would be an essential part of a successful recovery.

Children weren't allowed to listen to adults talk about the killings, and we were warned that we'd be punished if we were caught talking about it amongst ourselves. The adults— encouraged by our new president, Pasteur Bizimungu—were focusing on the future and doing all they could to repair the racial chasm that had been cut deep into the hearts of Rwandans. At the president's side was Vice President Paul Kagame, the man who had led the RPF, the rebel force that had sent the Interahamwe running for the hills. Side by side, President Bizimungu, a Hutu, and Vice President Kagame, a Tutsi, led and exemplified the new Rwanda, a country in which race was no longer a political factor—or a factor of *any* significance whatsoever.

To that end, we had also been issued new identity cards. Instead of being marked "Hutu" or "Tutsi," we were simply identified as "Rwandan." The identity cards that had once divided us and had ultimately cost hundreds of thousands of lives would now unite us all.

As for me, I was now a teenager, considered a man in most respects. My father had passed away, and I was doing all I could to help my mother and my older sister Mukamana to run our home. But one day my mum received some news that would send me on yet another journey. It would change me in ways I never could have imagined.

"Frederick, come sit down."

"Yes?"

"Your aunt Marceline's husband has been killed. I need you to go and see what you can do to help her."

My mother's sister Marceline lived in Gisenyi-town, a good five-hour trip. So I gathered some clothes and food, and my mother sent me off with a hug and a few Rwandan francs for bus fare. It was a three-hour walk across the hills to catch the bus in Kabaya. From there I would ride into Mukamira and catch another bus into Gisenyi.

In a way, I was looking forward to the adventure. Gisenyi is a beautiful town lying around the edge of Lake Kivu, the largest freshwater lake in Rwanda, which stretches west into the Congo. Historically, Gisenyi had been an attraction for the wealthy Americans and Europeans visiting Rwanda. Its pebbly sand beaches and tidal lake rivaled any pictures I'd seen of tourist destinations around the world. Luxurious hotels with aqua-blue pools and reclined lounge chairs sat on the shore of the lake, and sometimes you could see the white people in sunglasses reading a book by the pool. But the big glass doors with brass handles deterred poor village boys like me from even attempting to enter there.

From Gisenyi, you can also see the Nyiragongo volcano in the Congo rising up into the horizon. During the day, smoke can be seen wafting from the top, and if it's clear, you can also see the red glow burning through the night.

Although there had been talk of *abacengezi* in that area—the Interahamwe coming out of hiding in the Congo to infiltrate our country—our village, hours away in Ramba, had seen nothing to confirm those rumors.

It was on the second bus, from Mukamira to Gisenyi, that I noticed all of the roadblocks. But each time we stopped, the soldiers would talk to the bus driver through his window, maybe check the adults' identity cards to ensure they weren't infiltrators, and we would be on our way.

When we stopped again, some of the adults shuffled for their identity cards. I barely even looked up until someone whispered, "*Tugiye gupfa.*"

We're going to die.

From my window, about halfway back behind the driver, I couldn't really see the men. But it wouldn't be long before we all did.

"Off the bus!" a voice demanded.

One by one, eighteen of us filed out onto the narrow stone bridge, the only flat area between the green mountain above me and the misty valley below me. A few of the men stood ready with rifles, sending a clear message that if we tried to run, we wouldn't make it very far. As we exited the bus, even more men stepped out of the bushes and from behind the trees where they had been hiding. Now twenty to thirty men, all dressed in military uniforms mismatched with jeans or T-shirts, gathered around us and began shouting orders. But the one word that I heard the loudest was *abakada*. Traitors.

"Arms up!"

"Stand in a line!"

"Hands on your head!"

We didn't speak; we just obeyed as they came down the line, tying our arms behind our backs. I watched as they bound the woman in front of me, elbow to elbow, with green electrical cord. Then the man stepped toward me. As he forced my elbows together, it became more difficult to stand, to breathe. But I didn't move or make a sound as I felt the thin green wire cutting into my arms.

"Let's go!" another shouted. They prodded us with clubs and knives to walk down off the bridge and into the valley. We climbed up and down the mountain paths for hours, in silence only interrupted by the occasional whimper as someone lost her footing in the damp grass. At last, we arrived at their camp in Ruvuzananga, a small village in the Rwerere area, with makeshift buildings and hundreds of other people, both soldiers and even more prisoners.

I was surprised to see that some of the other "soldiers" were my age or maybe younger. They stood rigidly with cold eyes, guarding doorways and shouting at other prisoners. I wondered how long they had been there, how they could arrive at such a position, what had led them to carry such hatred at such a young age.

The soldiers and prisoners alike all seemed to watch casually as the men told us to sit down, pushing and kicking down any who didn't move quickly enough. Then they began to beat us. With spears, clubs, and sticks, they mercilessly beat us for hours on end. Fueled by an endless energy, they bloodied our faces, tore open our backs, and ripped the hope from our souls. They were finally freeing the anger that had been pent up for years as they waited, defeated, hiding in the Congo.

The Interahamwe had returned to finish their mission.

The next morning, we awoke to their shouts. Swollen,

scabbed, and still throbbing, we were forced to walk deeper into the hills. The Rwandan government had gotten word of the infiltrators' activity, and they were patrolling the area. Of course, from the main road, it was hard not to notice the disembodied hands and heads held high on wooden stakes left by the *abacengezi* as some sort of barbaric message of imminent doom for all Rwandans. Government soldiers had since been moving in, raiding their camps and making arrests—hence the increase in government roadblocks as we approached Gisenyi. But now, here, hidden high in the hills, there was little chance of government intervention. They would never find us.

When we stopped, well camouflaged by the lush canopy of eucalyptus trees, the men lined us up in a row.

"Take off all of your clothes," one demanded.

Of course, our arms were of no use, bound behind our backs, so we stepped and stumbled while the men ripped off clothing until we all stood naked. One woman had left her underwear on, so the man jerked it down and told her to kick it away. She obeyed, and he scooped it up, adding it to the bag of clothes he had gathered.

Then the leader turned to me. I'm not sure why he chose me. Because I was a teenage boy? Because I looked like a Hutu? Because I didn't have an identity card? I will never know. But I do know that I will never forget what he said next.

"I want you to kill all of these people."

He gestured toward them with his machete.

I stared at them, horrified.

"KILL these people!" This time he raised the machete at me.

I knew what would happen if I refused. Yet obeying the order meant I would become one of them—I would join their mission to kill the Tutsis and Tutsi-sympathizers of Rwanda. If I didn't obey him, I knew that I would die. But it didn't matter. The way I felt at that moment—exhausted, battered, humiliated—I was already dead.

four

how the killers
saved my life

*"You intended to harm me, but God intended it for good
to accomplish what is now being done,
the saving of many lives."*
—Genesis 50:20 niv

I looked at the man with the machete. "My God won't let me do that."

He stared back with almost a smile. "We will use him to send a message," he said coldly to those standing by. Then within seconds, those men with machetes and clubs began to unleash their evil on the others. This time, I knew it would be more than a beating. This time, I knew we would die.

With blades raised high, the men hacked away at those with whom I had shared a bus only a day before. The men—fathers, brothers, village leaders—were all reduced to gasping, crumpled corpses within minutes.

They dragged the women a few feet away. You know what happened to them—right in front of us, with no shame, and with the same anger that powered the machetes and clubs. We would later learn that these acts were a form of weaponry in itself, throughout the genocide and beyond. The men who were HIV-positive would rape the women ruthlessly with the intention of spreading their disease not only to the mothers, but to the potential children they may come to carry, leaving behind the effects of their malevolence for years to come.

When the killers finished with the women, they chopped and clubbed away at them until the mothers, daughters, wives fell limp, like abandoned rag dolls, into a cloud of red earth.

And then they all looked to me.

Bloodied bodies lay all around me. Still bound at the elbows, my face and body were swollen beyond recognition from yesterday's beatings that had continued well into the morning. I sat defenseless, on my knees, waiting to be the messenger for their sinister missive.

"Take him to the slaughtering area," one man said.

I knew exactly where he meant. I had seen it earlier near the camp. It was where they ceremoniously made examples of unruly prisoners. To them, it was more than sending a message; it was a game.

I was jerked to my feet and shoved in the general direction of their death ring. As we approached, one of the men kicked me from behind, and I fell to my knees.

"Now, who has a good machete?" I can still see the man, wearing a gray shirt under a long coat with a hat pulled down to his brow.

"I do," a voice volunteered from behind me.

The man in the gray shirt pushed his foot against my back.

"Stay down," he said and cut between my elbows with the machete. Intense pain rushed through my shoulders as my arms resumed a normal position. He had cut the cord that bound my elbows together, but I could still see the green electrical wire circling each arm, held in place by my skin that had swollen around it.

The freedom didn't last long. The man then tied each hand to a small, wooden platform, and I closed my eyes. I felt two heavy feet step onto my back and stand there as another put one foot on each of my legs.

With tensed shoulders, I waited, expecting the blow to be to my head. It was one of the ways they sent "messages" to the people, hanging heads on stakes by the road to Gisenyi-town. There was a story of how they had forced their way into a woman's home and demanded food. When she replied, honestly, that she had none, they called her a traitor, accused her of supporting the Rwandan government, and made an example of her. They hung her head on a tall wooden stake out by the road to ward off any other potential "traitors."

However, when the man swung the machete, the blade hit my arm, about halfway between my elbow and my wrist. The first blow cut the skin, but the bones of a teenage boy are not at all brittle. They stand up well against a battle-worn man slinging a dulled machete. Still, evil does not so easily relent. Each hack of the machete landed in a slightly different spot, creating a series of deep gashes up and down my arm.

I gathered all the strength left within me and began to beg. "Please, please sir, just leave me a thumb!" Losing my hands would be a death sentence in itself. Planting is how we survive. Without hands, I couldn't plant. I couldn't dig. I couldn't harvest.

My cries were lost amidst the repeated thud of a dull machete against cracking bones and the cheers of the other men. They shrieked and laughed as blood began to spurt across the platform at them; they scattered like children running from "it" in a game of tag. One by one, my hands fell motionless to the ground, and the men continued to jeer and point, as with each beat of my heart, two steady streams of crimson shot across the platform into the grass.

It had happened so quickly, but then time stopped. I saw the trees around me, the maniacal men, my two red-soaked, mangled stumps, and my hands lying there on the ground, covered in blood. Someone was jerking me to my feet, kicking me forward.

Two boys appeared.

"You two, grab some stones!" the gray-shirted man yelled at the boys stumbling onto the horrid scene. "Finish him off—then leave him for the dogs." The killers, obviously exhausted by their marathon of macabre, were finished with me.

Gravity and weak-kneed steps kept me moving further down the path. I walked past the two staring boys. I walked and yet no one chased me. I walked down the steep hill, deep into the trees.

I was finally free.

I walked that way—with freshly severed arms, losing life with each heartbeat—for five kilometers, up and down the steep hills of Rwanda. That same strength that had carried my family to the refugee camp and back would carry me now. It would again save my life.

Then there, against the rich pink and purple of the dusky African sky, I saw them. Two sisters, on their way home from church, approached me. They struggled in vain to hide their shocked repulsion of my appearance—my handless arms, my naked body caked in dried blood. The older sister untied the shawl from around her shoulders and carefully wrapped the fabric around my waist. I collapsed against her.

With a sister on each side, together we walked the remaining two kilometers, trying to navigate the three interlocked figures through the thick brush on the way to their home. It was a small, mud-bricked house much like my own family's, but unlike ours nestled high in the hills, theirs was right on the main road in a small town. The girls helped me inside and built a fire to keep me warm. They made a pallet for me by the fire and found some cloth to wrap around my arms. I awkwardly, gratefully positioned myself to rest there in the home of these strangers, my saviors.

Somewhere along the way, my arms had stopped the profuse bleeding. There was no pain—my entire body was numb. It was difficult to focus on anything but the beat of my heart and the flicker of the fire.

The sisters sat there, still wide-eyed, watching as I faded away to a deep sleep. Those warm, dark faces lit by the glowing fire would be the last thing I would remember for a very long time.

I would later be told about the next morning: how the girls had flagged down a military truck and asked the men to help, how the soldiers could offer no medical care but could get me to the hospital, how the soldiers had risked their lives with the decision to load me in the back of their truck. Others would tell me how the brave men carried me through the Interahamwe raid fence, where only soldiers could pass, where few civilians dared to go, and how they protected me as they drove through gunfire to the hospital in Gisenyi.

I would also learn how those green electrical cords that bound me, and the fierce anger with which they were tied, had saved my life. They had been tied so tightly that they had not only restricted the movement of my arms, but later slowed the loss of blood. What those men had meant to harm me, God had used for good.

Still, it would be a long time before I learned any of this.

For now, I would sleep.

five

what will never be

"Long enough, God—you've ignored me long enough.
I've looked at the back of your head long enough.
Long enough I've carried this ton of trouble,
lived with a stomach full of pain."
—Psalm 13:1–2 MSG

I awoke to a strange face in a strange place.

Someone was touching my arm. Through blurred vision, I saw a woman; from behind her came a blinding light and a warm, moist breeze. I blinked. From all directions, I heard voices, so many voices, some crying, some calming. I tried to speak but couldn't seem to swallow the stone in my throat. My body was heavy, weighted down by an invisible force so strong, I felt that I would break through my cot any minute and sink into the middle of the earth. I tried to fight against it, to lift my hands or just a finger.

Then I looked down.

I saw gauzy white stumps where my hands once were. And I remembered.

It was too much. I closed my eyes.

The pelting of rain on metal woke me again.

Is it already the rainy season? I must have been sleeping for days.

Pain tore through my arms. I looked down at them and saw hands holding rust-stained gauze. The woman belonging to the hands looked at me, a bit startled. "Well, hello there. I'm Fitina. It's good to finally see you."

She must have read the questions on my face. "You're in a hospital in Gisenyi. You were—you were hurt. You've been here for about six months."

Six months! I have been sleeping for six months? Is that even possible?

Over the next few weeks, I would learn what had happened to me and to my country while I had been sleeping. For the hospital, I was just one of many machete victims brought in during that time. The hospital was getting sometimes as many as a hundred a day before the Interahamwe infiltrators were pushed out, once and for all, by the RPF. It was truly the end of those genocidaires, the last time they would rise up, with any significance, against our country.

The genocide was truly over. Rwanda was finally safe.

While the fighting subsided, my home had been a relatively large hospital situated on a rolling hill in Gisenyi. Several separate buildings housed different departments. There was a surgery department, a critical care unit, administrative buildings, a morgue, and an area that housed the doctors' offices for the walk-in clinic. A storeroom and utility room sat atop a hill on the back of the property, where workers would wash the hospital's linens by hand and hang them to dry. A large open-air kitchen, with two wood stoves flanked by concrete benches, sat near the storeroom. My bed was one of many in a large open-air platform with a tin roof. There were plastic walls that could be used for enclosures, but most of the time they were left open for the air to circulate.

Of the victims still recovering at the hospital, I certainly wasn't the worst. Others had presented with a missing leg or a stomach slashed open. And those were just the ones who, by some miracle, had made it to the hospital.

My arms had stopped bleeding by the time I arrived at the hospital, more than twelve hours after the incident. However, the fabric wrapped around my arms had been plastered over the open wound by the drying blood, and it took hours of soaking and careful cutting away to remove the makeshift bandages. The hospital surgeon was able, through a series of surgeries, to properly trim and close arteries, muscles, and nerves, and to cover the open wound with my own skin. He also removed that green electrical wire that was embedded in my skin, the wire that had saved my life.

Still, those caring for me weren't so sure of my survival. After a while, they lost hope that I would ever wake up, and deep down they knew it might be better if I didn't. They had seen the bitter anger that had plagued many a victim. They knew a young man with no hands would have little hope for a life with any dignity or quality whatsoever. Disabled children were burdens to their families—mouths to feed with little to offer in return.

Of course, this wasn't something discussed openly, but I knew of mentally handicapped children hidden away in their homes, left alone all day while the parents worked at the market or in the tea fields. I had seen physically disabled children in shredded clothes, with filth-crusted faces, begging for food—or *anything* really—alone, on the side of the road. No one had to say it. I knew it as soon as the machete struck: the loss of my hands would forever change my life.

Those changes were evident almost immediately.

From the moment I woke up until I fell asleep at night— every single day—I was so painfully aware of what those men had taken from me. Everything I used my hands for in the past, which was pretty much *everything*, I now needed help to do. As kind as they were to me, the overwhelmed nurses and doctors caring for bleeding, dying, diseased people could hardly give priority to assisting a relatively healthy boy in getting dressed or bathed. Even after I was able to dress myself, for the most part, buttons and zippers proved impossible to manipulate. And I learned quickly that asking a nearby woman to help fasten my pants was never a good idea.

It was a few weeks before the doctors allowed me to have solid food; it was probably here that I felt the full extent of my disability. Food was hard enough to come by for the patients, especially those like me, with no family around. Typically, family and friends would bring food in to supplement the hospital's staple of feed corn served daily. But no one even knew I was here.

My mother had no way of knowing that I didn't arrive at my aunt's, and my aunt probably never knew that I was coming to help her. Although by this time, six months later, my mother would have begun to wonder. Now that the hospital knew my name and where I came from, there was hope that news of what had happened would travel back to my village, to my mother, and she would come to bring me home. However, as much as I longed to be home again with my family, I wasn't entirely sure that I wanted them to see how I had been changed.

And for now, the fact remained: I was on my own.

I would do what I must to survive, and for the time being, that meant finding food. When other patients had leftovers from what their families had brought them, I would gladly finish off their dinners. People from the local churches would also come by every so often and distribute bread to each bed. And soon I found other patients in my same situation, and together we would gather food to share among us.

It was then that I also had my first experience as a beggar. I had seen it done plenty of times before, and it looked simple enough. Though beggars were beggars, they still were obviously able to subsist on the food they garnered through the practice. And I was more than willing to give it a try, to do everything I could to make my own way.

I walked with some of the other patients, members of my food team, to the edge of the bustling road that runs by the hospital. In Rwanda, especially at that time, there were very few cars, but there was an endless stream of traffic. The majority of people were on foot, while some pushed bicycles laden with goods, and fewer still were taxied on the backs of motorcycles.

The ends of my arms were still thick with bandages as I held them out to indicate my need. I tried not to think about it too much—about what would happen if someone I knew saw me, standing there, reduced to begging for food. My family was never wealthy, by any measurement of wealth, but we always had enough. We always took care of ourselves. And now, here I was, depending on others to take care of me—in so many ways. Long after I had escaped those evil men, they were still rendering me helpless and humiliated.

But I was hungry. And I wasn't alone. I had to find food, and I knew that everything I gathered, I would share with my new friends.

Hundreds of people passed, many of them carrying loads of bananas or chickens or avocadoes to and from the market. But only a few ever looked my way. Even fewer would offer anything to help.

Then a man approached with a basket full of cabbages. "Here you go, son," he said, reaching one out to me.

I reached out to take the cool, rubbery head, and it rolled along my arm before splatting into the dirt at my bare feet. I tried to pick it up, but the result was more of a soccer game with my arms and the cabbage, rolling it around but never getting it off the ground. As a result, after what felt like endless hours of my first day as a beggar, my bandages were now caked in dirt, my arms were throbbing, and all I had earned was a bruised cabbage that I couldn't pick up and take back with me.

That's when I realized: I wasn't even able to be a beggar. The lowest form of earning a living, the least respectful position in society—I had been reduced to even lower than that.

What hope would that leave for me? What in this world would I have to look forward to?

＊

I spent the next several weeks thinking about the past, asking God why He had let me live, wondering how I had arrived at this lowly place in my life. I had been raised, for the most part, by two hardworking parents who loved me, surrounded by playful brothers and sisters, always working together as a family to get by. Ours was a typical Rwandan home: a humble, three-room, mud-brick house with a tiled roof. The only exception was that in many homes, the cooking fire was in the corner of the main room to provide warmth while meals were cooked. But we had a small kitchen outside, where Mum would have more space to prepare and cook our meals over the fire.

Even today, this is the typical cooking method in Rwanda, over an open fire. The hospitals, hotels, and many restaurants use wood fires for cooking too. This gives the whole country of Rwanda a unique, ever-present aroma of burning wood.

The main room held a small hand-hewn table and two small benches where we would eat or invite visitors to sit. Each of us had our mats to sleep on, but during the day, they were rolled up and placed in the corner to make space. We had a small pen just outside the home where we would keep a couple of goats, or if times were good, a cow.

Like many Rwandans, my father and mother were both farmers, raising what we needed to feed our family and taking any abundance to the market to trade or sell. We grew beans, cassava, sweet potatoes, and had some banana trees around the house. We sometimes had a cow and always had goats and chickens.

When I was young, my parents and our oldest sister, Valerie, would leave the house around four in the morning to go to the farm, about an hour away from our house. The young kids, including myself, would stay home and take the animals to graze. We would also draw water for the animals, for cooking, and for bathing. I was the oldest boy out of nine children. Although some of us went to school, four of my brothers and sisters didn't; they would stay home to help our parents around the house and farm. That was common then and even today. School was a luxury that some families just couldn't afford for all of their children.

Each day after returning home from the farm, my mother and sister would cook food they'd harvested, usually cassava or potatoes, and my dad would go to the bar to recap the day with his friends over a glass or two of banana beer. While my mother and sister started the fire and washed and chopped potatoes, the younger sisters would clean up around the house, washing dishes or clothes in a small plastic basin, scrubbing them against a bar of soap. While they were in the house, we boys ventured out to collect firewood, but it wasn't uncommon for a game of soccer to break out while we were "collecting wood."

In the evenings, my father would return home, and we'd all sit there together, listening to his stories while the smell of simmering potatoes tempted our taste buds. His stories often continued long after dinner, entertaining us well into the night. Everyone seemed to love that about him—his enchanting way of weaving a story and spreading joy, especially during those times when there was little to be joyful about.

Sundays were always special days in our family. We would wake up early as usual, but not to do our chores. Everyone got washed up and put on their clean clothes. We didn't have an iron, so our best clothes always hung neatly in the corner of our room to keep them from being wrinkled. When I was a child, we attended a large Catholic church, with more than five hundred people. In order to make it to the eight o'clock service, we started our two-and-a-half-hour walk well before the sun had burned the mist out of the mountains. By the time we got to church, our shoes were often caked with red Rwandan mud from traveling for miles along the hilly dirt paths. So part of the Sunday ritual included stopping outside the church as we arrived, along with the rest of the congregation, and cleaning off our shoes with a rag we had brought along for that very purpose. The music and message of the Sunday sermon always refreshed our souls for whatever the coming week would hold.

For my mother, it was important that we all work together and spend time together as a family. As much as I appreciated that, I would always be thrilled when my parents would let me venture off to spend time with my grandmother; in fact, I would often look for reasons to go. Her house was in another rural village, about a two-hour walk from our own. My parents would usually send me with a bag of potatoes for her, and once there, I would do my usual chores, fetching water and wood and grass for the cows. But I just liked to be around her. At night, she always told me stories about her childhood, what they did when she was a girl, how they weaved baskets and mats from grasses and leaves.

She would tell me what times were like when Rwanda still had a *mwami*, or king, and how he would award gifts of cows and land to the villagers. For entertainment, the king would often call for dancers and singers, and my grandfather was apparently quite talented at both. After one of my grandfather's performances, the king was so pleased that he presented him with a tract of land. My grandmother lived on that land until the genocide, long after my grandfather had passed.

My grandmother, too, had developed quite a reputation in her own right. Even in her old age, when I would visit, people were still flocking to her from all over to hear what she could tell them about their future. Men and women alike would bring her gifts of money, passion fruit, or honey in exchange for her wisdom. Many were well aware of her standing as a wise prophet. Others approached her skeptically at first, but would often return with an even larger gift because what my grandmother told them had come true, saving them from trouble or guiding them to make an important decision.

My grandmother even saw her own future. She had told me several times as a child how she wouldn't die in Rwanda, which seemed so odd to me because she had never left her village that I had known of. But sure enough, years later when the genocide began to tear through our country and we all fled to refugee camps, my grandmother packed up what she could carry and headed west into the Congo, never to return again.

My childhood was a place of warm, welcoming memories. As a child, I knew that our country was not rich but beautiful, not luxurious but lush, not a superpower but safe. It was all we needed, all we wanted, and so much more.

That place seemed so far away now. Instead of finding solace in the memories of home, they tore at my very soul, reminding me of what would never be again, taunting me with the happiness and wholeness I had lost that day. It was as if I had exited the bus that day into a foreign, evil world full of strange, angry faces, where I stepped down from being a young man full of promise to a helpless beggar fraught with despair.

Even here at the hospital, this place of healing, insults were hurled. Of course, many people were helpful and encouraging, but they did little to ease the sting of reality that the others reminded me of. "You're useless. You'd be better off a dead man," some told me. One nurse joked, "You can't even sing where I could take you home to entertain my children." Others were so frightened by my disfigurement, they would scatter when I came around, just as the men had done the day they took my hands.

Now I knew without a doubt: I would never again be that young man my mother depended on, the one she trusted and dispatched to help the family when someone was in need. I was more like Louise, the young woman who now wandered the hospital grounds, wailing incoherently. Her mind and the life within it had been stripped away by the toil of incessant violence. I was envious of her in a way. At least for her, there were no memories of joys past to serve as stark comparisons to the present torture, no spectrum to show her how far the pendulum had swung.

For me, I remembered it all, and I knew.

There was no hope.

six

trying to die

"No one can know what such a loss means unless he has suffered a similar catastrophe. In the twinkling of an eye, life's fondest hopes seemed dead. I was the prey of despair. What could the world hold for a maimed, crippled man?!"
—JAMES E. HANGER, FOUNDER OF HANGER PROSTHETICS

The screams woke me, as they usually did.

The doctors and nurses were making their rounds, cleaning and dressing the wounds in my area. Even where we were, out in the open air, the cries of the patients reverberated as if on tin walls. For all of us waiting our turns, it was by far the worst part of any day.

There were always about twenty people ahead of me, screaming out each time the nurse would remove the bandage and clean the wound beneath. Some nurses were sympathetic, wetting the bandages, pulling slowly, and speaking softly to ease our minds. Others seemed to enjoy inflicting pain, yanking dry bandages, skin and all. Either way, the pain was unbearable.

My friends and I made up songs to distract us as the doctors came down the line. We would sing and laugh almost loudly enough to drown out the sounds of agony that grew closer by the moment. Like the stories of my father, the songs soothed my soul as we waited. But even bittersweet moments like those were scarce.

One morning, I had barely gotten to sleep when I awoke to those screams. I had been up all night writhing in pain, unable to get relief regardless of what position I was in or how I rested my arms. In the light of the new day, already exhausted, I was decimated by the cries of fellow patients, feeling their pain again and again with each cry, cries that seemed to never end. When they did end, it only meant one thing: it was my turn.

And it was too much.

I had been through enough. I had fled my home, hiked the bloody hills of Rwanda, watched the death of my country, lost my hands and my means of survival—all in the course of a few years. I had no more left to give, no more life left within me. I had fought as long as I possibly could.

Exhausted and empty, I decided.

It was over.

When the nurse came by that day, I opened my mouth wide and let him put in the pills as usual. As soon as he turned to the next bed, I silently dropped them onto my bandaged arm and hid them away. Over the next few days, I tried to hide the resurging pain and swelling in my arms.

"Have you taken your medicine today?" a nurse asked.

"Yes," I nodded a little too enthusiastically.

No one ever noticed. No one had time to.

After about a week of this, I had amassed quite an arsenal

of pills and capsules, folding the tiny pellets up in a makeshift envelope I had made out of paper. I wasn't sure what each of them were—some pain pills, some antibiotics—but I knew that enough of them would do the job.

I spent those last days convincing myself this was the only way. I soaked in the stench of all the tragedies I had witnessed and experienced over the last few years. I berated myself into believing that my death would affect no one but myself.

No one would even know I was gone. My mother, my family—I was certain—had already dismissed me as dead. And it would be better to leave it that way.

In fact, in many ways, my death would do nothing but good for those around me. For the overwhelmed nurses and doctors, I would be one less patient to dress and feed. For the hospital, I would be an empty bed, one more outstanding bill that would never be paid. For Rwanda, I would be one less beggar. *No, I wouldn't even be that.* For Rwanda, I would be one less incapable human hidden away to rot in his home. One less mouth to feed. One less burden. One less disabled man to bathe and dress and support throughout the term of his useless existence.

Yes, this would be good for everyone.

Of course, I didn't know that my mother would soon hear the news of my condition and immediately come looking for me. I didn't know that other people like me would need an advocate to teach them and inspire them and show them the way. I didn't know that God already had enormous plans for these two hand-less arms.

I had no imagination for what lay ahead. There, within my limited human mind, I allowed my past and my current circumstances to disillusion me into a state of complete hopelessness. And I took it upon myself to be the god of my fate.

The next morning, the nurses and doctors made their rounds as they always did. But my mind was silent. My body was numb. Holding that little paper shell between my elbows, I lifted it to my mouth and poured it in like buckshot, swallowing mouthful after mouthful of the medicine that I hoped would finally bring me relief.

I pulled my blankets up to shroud my soon-lifeless body.

And I waited to die.

But I didn't.

My mouth was dry, and it was difficult to speak. I was weak and dizzy.

But when the nurse came to my bed, she treated me as usual, and walked away.

Maybe it takes more time, I reasoned.

I waited all day, and still no relief came.

Maybe it will happen in my sleep.

The next morning, the light woke me as it always did.

What happened? What did I do wrong? I even failed at killing myself?! Maybe the hospital is giving us expired pills. Or maybe I am dead!

As the day wore on, I knew. I was still very much alive.

And maybe, just maybe, there was a reason why.

A few nights later, as we sometimes did, my friends and I sang from the hymnal that visitors had left for the patient beside me. She was very sick; she couldn't speak, and we weren't even sure she could hear or see us. Still, we often borrowed her hymnal to find the words of the songs that reminded us of our churches at home.

One of our favorites was a song that we had often sung in church. The legend behind the song is that a young girl's parents wanted her to marry the king against her will. To ease her suffering, she wrote this song and vowed to sing it until she died. In an odd way, I could relate to that story. And as we sang it this time, I let the words sink in. For the first time in a long time, I listened.

Njye nd'umukristo icyo n'ikintu gihumuriz' umutima wanjye.

I am a Christian, and it consoles my soul.

Kinyibagiza ibyago byose nkumva nduhuwe n'umwami yesu.

It makes me forget all my pain and sufferings when I feel the support of Jesus.

("Njye Ndi Umukristo")

As I listened to the words and the voices around me, I realized that I was truly not alone in my suffering. I realized that dying was not the answer, and that maybe God had a plan for even me. Although I had been reduced to nothing by society's standards, set up to fail by human guidelines, maybe there was another perspective that I had not considered.

I began looking for answers.

And one day soon after, I found them.

Flipping through my Bible, I stopped at a psalm, and I heard my heart speaking as I read:

> *O Lord, God of my salvation,*
> *I have cried out day and night before You.*
> *Let my prayer come before You;*
> *Incline Your ear to my cry.*
>
> *For my soul is full of troubles,*
> *And my life draws near to the grave.*
> *I am counted with those who go down to the pit;*
> *I am like a man who has no strength,*
> *Adrift among the dead,*
> *Like the slain who lie in the grave,*
> *Whom You remember no more,*
> *And who are cut off from Your hand.*
>
> *You have laid me in the lowest pit,*
> *In darkness, in the depths.*
> *Your wrath lies heavy upon me,*
> *And You have afflicted me with all Your waves.*
> *You have put away my acquaintances far from me;*
> *You have made me an abomination to them;*

I am shut up, and I cannot get out;
My eye wastes away because of affliction.

LORD, I have called daily upon You;
I have stretched out my hands to You.
Will You work wonders for the dead?
Shall the dead arise and praise You?
Shall Your lovingkindness be declared in the grave?
Or Your faithfulness in the place of destruction?
Shall Your wonders be known in the dark?
And Your righteousness in the land of forgetfulness?

(Ps. 88:1–12 NKJV)

Could He? Could He work wonders for me? Should I arise from the dead and praise Him, declare His lovingkindness? Can I find a way to feel His faithfulness in this place of destruction? Will His wonders come to light here in the dark, His righteousness be remembered where we have all forgotten?

All at once, a radiating warmth filled my core, then washed over me, bringing every hair follicle, every skin cell, and every sensation to life. My eyes were opened. My soul was aware. My ears and my heart were tuned to listen.

And I knew the answer.

Yes.

seven

learning to
live again

"For this very purpose I have raised you up,
that I may show My power in you, and that My
name may be declared in all the earth."
—ROMANS 9:17 NKJV

For a while, I felt extreme guilt for trying to end my life, for lacking the faith to face another day.

I had ignored the many ways God had spared me: how He had carried me safely home from my sister's house, how He had walked us safely to the refugee camp and back, how He had kept us safe and hidden as the killers swept through our countryside, how He was restoring our country and continuing to provide for my family even after our earthly father was gone.

And when I needed Him most, He gave me, one young boy, the courage to stand up to a gang of grown men and refuse to reduce myself to their level of evil. He had spared my head and allowed only my hands to be taken. He had stunned those two little boys long enough for me to pass, keeping them from stoning me, from finishing me off. He had sent two sisters to carry me to their home, where a truck full of brave military men would pass the next day. He guarded that truck so that we could safely pass through to the hospital. He placed a skillful surgeon at my bedside. And even when I had lost all hope of living, when I had given up on Him and myself, He had sent yet another miracle to ensure my survival.

One word echoed throughout my body and soul.

Why?

Why He chose me, why He even cared that a young Rwandan boy was alive, I couldn't fathom.

But I knew this: I would spend the rest of my life figuring it out.

From that point forward, I resolved to do all I could to make the absolute most of this life that God had given me. I was here for a purpose, to somehow bring light to all of this darkness, to let God's glory shine through all of this suffering, to make everyone see that no matter what evil men meant to harm us, God would use it for His good.

I wasn't going to stop, I wasn't going to back down, until that purpose was fulfilled.

But first, I had to get out of this hospital.

It had been six months since I had woken to find myself in a hospital bed. It had been a year since I had lost my hands. The swelling in my arms was gone, along with the major risk of infection. Through multiple surgeries, the trauma to my arms had been hidden as best as possible. At the ends of my arms, skin now covered the bones and muscle beneath—rounded perfectly, taut and smooth, almost like the point of an elbow. To look at them, if you didn't know better, you would think that I was born that way, that God had formed my arms Himself.

With all the progress that I had made, I was still a long way from being independent, and even farther from being able to fulfill any grand purpose of helping others. I tried not to dwell on that; I instead reminded myself of how far I had come and how I was finally ready to move on.

As I prepared to leave the hospital, I was beyond excited to get back home, but I did not look forward to leaving my friends. Some had healed quickly and had already gone home to their own lives, but others had been there, by my side, for months. Several of us would stay up and talk long into the night, laughing and telling stories from our childhood and happier times, especially when one of us was nagged from our sleep by pain or discomfort. Their friendship was an immeasurable comfort when I was hurting or feeling alone, a healing presence within itself, and their cheerful faces were a welcome distraction from the diseased and dying all around us. I would miss them; there was no doubt. I didn't want to admit it, but I was quite apprehensive about facing my new reality without them.

Yet there was no stopping that day from coming. Before I knew it, the staff and my friends gathered to send me off, and I stepped out onto that same street where I had my first experience as a beggar. I followed the directions the nurse gave me to the Ngoboka Transit Center, a home for "unaccompanied children," children like me.

The center was run by Save the Children, a group from the United States that was helping children displaced by the genocide, caring for them until they found their families. At the center, I was welcomed and cared for, given a bed, and assisted in my daily care. I was one of the older kids, but I required the same care as the little ones. As much as they cared for me, I knew this was just a temporary home.

I still longed to see my mother again and often imagined what that day would be like. She surely thought I had been killed by now, so just seeing me alive again would be an incredible surprise for her. I would run to her, and she would wrap those long arms around me, holding me as I told her everything that had happened. Even without hands, I would be whole again, just to see my mother, to return to my family, to my home there high on the hill. Together, again, we would make it through.

Until then, I would wait.

After a few weeks there, a lady in the center called to me.

"Frederick, you have a visitor! Out front . . ."

Ah, one of my dear hospital friends, I thought, quickly making my way to the front of the building. *Who else would know I am here?*

But then I saw her. Standing there with a basket of bananas, looking around a bit nervously, my mother had finally found me.

She stiffened a bit when I ran toward her, but as I melted into her arms, she collapsed against me in muffled, shaking sobs.

I was home.

We sat down to talk, and she held the bananas out toward me.

So much had changed since she had seen me last. I laughed and shrugged as I held out my arms.

Embarrassed, she pulled the bananas back quickly and slowly broke one off the bunch. As she peeled back each section, tears fell in shimmery streaks on her ashen cheeks.

Handing the banana to me, she began, "I—I had heard that you lost your arms *and* your legs."

"No, no." I laughed again. "I have my legs!" I kicked them wildly from beneath the bench.

She forced a smile, looking down at them, and whispered, "I was just so happy to hear that you were alive."

"I am alive," I agreed.

Silence sat between us as I fumbled each bite of the banana. I knew there was something else.

"Your sister—" She looked up at me, then down to my arms, hiding a wince. "She—well, she went out one day and didn't make it back." She covered her face, barely getting the words out before a bitter weeping took over.

I didn't know what to say; I had never seen my mother cry like this.

Then she wailed more loudly, "Mukamana, my child! Why her? Why did she die and *you*—you survive?" She dropped her hands and pierced me with an accusatory look.

"What will you *do*? How will you live like *this*?!" She motioned her hands toward my lack of them.

My mother's words cut right through me. And yet I understood.

Hadn't I thought the very same thing? How could I blame her? She had lost the oldest daughter she had living at home, the only other adult to help with the farming and the house and the children since my father had died. And in return, she had gained what? Me? Barely a man, with no hands? I couldn't even eat a banana without her help.

I looked down at her dusty feet, the thin soles of her sandals.

"I'm sorry," I said. And I meant it.

"Look . . ." She sniffed and swatted at her cheeks. "I can't stay here tonight. But I'll be back in the morning."

She sat the bananas on the bench beside me, hugged me lightly, and picked up her basket. She was gone.

I barely slept that night. I stared at the ceiling as the hopelessness crept in. It was so quiet that I could hear my heartbeat, the throb of blood rushing through my veins.

And I remembered: God has saved me for a purpose. I am *alive*.

Still, I wondered what this would mean for me, for my family. I couldn't burden my mother any more than she was already. The way she looked at my arms, I knew it would hurt her just to be around me. I had to do what was best for everyone.

So the next morning, when my mother came, I informed her of my decision. "I'm going to stay here for a little while."

She sighed and nodded.

"I have everything I need here, and they can teach me to take care of myself."

"I didn't mean—" she began.

"I know." I looked directly into her eyes. "This will be best for everyone."

She shook her head and reached for me, wrapping me in her arms. I relished the warmth, the scent of my mother, knowing that it could be the last time she held me as her child.

We spent the rest of the day together, catching up on family and friends and what had happened since I'd left. We laughed, remembering my father's stories and times when the whole family was together, when Valerie and Mukamana were still there to tattle on me and take care of me. But we both knew that was the past, and the future was waiting.

She gave me one last lingering hug, and I walked her to the road.

"I'll be fine," I said, searching her eyes. Then I knew she would be too.

Time went by slowly there at the center.

At first it was obvious that everyone was afraid of me—afraid to ask questions, afraid of hurting me, and maybe just afraid of being around someone different, a person with no hands. But eventually, curiosity and compassion got the best of them, especially the kids. They found ways to help me and began to ask questions.

I struggled daily with the most basic tasks. I could clumsily feed myself fruits and breads, but I couldn't use a fork. Since our meals consisted mostly of rice and beans and soupy vegetables, the other kids would feed me most of my meals. They also helped to bathe and dress me, which was completely mortifying for a teenage boy. I eventually joined them in playing around too. I would kick ball with the kids my age, but held myself back as a spectator for most of the real games. The biggest disappointment was that I still was not able to care for myself, to live independently. I still needed the help of others simply to survive.

When I would take my discouragement to God, the answer was always the same.

Just keep trying.

After a few months, I learned that my one independent choice—to stay there at the center—would also succumb to the will of others. The center had found homes for most of the children there and was closing. I would be returned home to my family. It was a success for the center, but for me it felt like failure.

I rode in silence to my village, watching as the hills and homes became more familiar as we drew closer. When we approached the church in my village, my mother was there waiting with my little brother and sister. They hid behind her as the van pulled up, but couldn't resist peeking around to see me step out of the big machine and watch it lumbering away down the narrow, winding road.

Home quickly felt like home again. Nothing had really changed around the house itself, and everyone pretended that nothing had changed with me either. My mum had told my siblings that I had lost my hands so my appearance wouldn't startle them, but their curiosity often got the best of them as they eyed my arms or rubbed the ends as they reached to hold my hand.

It never bothered me. I would make sure they were watching as I pulled an avocado from the tree. I'd toss them a ball or rub their heads playfully to help us all grow used to the sight and function of my new "hands."

As in any small village, my story circulated around ours

quickly. I began to notice hands shooting up to cover whispering mouths as I passed. Children would stop in their tracks and stare slack-jawed before their mothers shooed them past me. I already knew what the people were saying, and sometimes they made little effort to conceal it.

"How does he eat?"

"Can he even take a bath?"

"His poor mother must have to dress him."

One lady on the street even broke down crying just at the sight of me. After a while, I realized that my missing hands were more than evidence of the trauma I had experienced; they were a reminder of the violence that had traumatized all of us.

For a while, I continued to be the whispered hush of the village, and I knew things could never be normal as long as the whole village was tiptoeing around my family and me. Slowly, as time passed, I became ready to speak, and the people became ready to listen. I started to share my story, and as I did, fears were calmed, tensions eased.

It seemed that talking about my wounds brought healing for us all.

eight

finding home

*"Before the genocide, there wasn't a
word for orphan in Rwanda;
it just didn't happen."*
—CHARLENE JENDRY, FOUNDING MEMBER OF PIC

As much as I tried, I soon realized that I would never be able to succeed back at home in my village.

A planter with no hands is hardly a planter. When my mother was out laboring on the farm, doing the job of two men, I wasn't even able to do the job of a child. When I simply tried to perform my childhood task of fetching the water, I found that I could no longer lift an empty jerrican to my head, much less fill and carry a full one. I had tried to help keeping the animals, but I couldn't hold the rope or pour the feed. No matter what I did, in trying to assist in the basic daily chores, I only created more work for everyone. Plus, I still needed help caring for myself. My family barely generated enough food and income to survive as it was, and I was only making things more difficult, causing us all to fall further behind.

I had exhausted all of my options there. It seemed that there was nothing I could do in a village of planters and farmers to generate any income, to help support my family, much less eventually support myself. And there was one thing I knew for sure: this was not what God had planned for me, to be a helpless burden on my already overwhelmed family. As much as I hated to leave them again, I knew that there were more options back in Gisenyi than in my rural village in Ramba.

What if I moved back to Gisenyi? I thought and began making plans to do so. I knew that if I told my family, they would feel bad about it, as if they were doing something to make me feel unwelcome. I knew that they would only focus on me more and try harder to help me. I didn't want them to try to stop me or talk me out of it. I also didn't want them to worry about me when I left.

Often I would tell them, "One day, I'm going to return to Gisenyi, to find work there." Although they never seemed to take me very seriously, I said it enough so that when I left, they would realize where I had gone.

One Sunday morning, I knew it was time. I placed some clean clothes in a small bag. I slipped on the shoes that didn't tie, the kind I could put on myself, and I walked to the door.

"I'm headed to church," I called to my mum and quickly walked away before she could reply.

Once in Gisenyi, I realized how foolish my plan had been—or more accurately, my lack of a plan. I had left home with nothing but a couple of extra shirts. I had no money, no food, and no place to stay.

The smell of food lured me off the street and into a restaurant.

"Can I help you? Are you looking for something?" a woman asked. She owned the restaurant and was known throughout Gisenyi as Mama Chakura (meaning "Mama Food"). The restaurant sat on the shore of Lake Kivu. The building that housed the kitchen and restrooms was closest to the road, while pavilions and thatch-roofed tables were scattered across the rest of the property, overlooking the lake. Huge, whole fish, pulled from the waters of Lake Kivu and grilled over an open fire, were topped with onions and fresh limes and served with a side of deep-fried potatoes.

My stomach cried out for relief. "I've come here from Ramba looking for work. Do you know where I could sleep for the night?"

"Sit down, son," she said, handing me a piece of bread. She looked me over, noting my arms and the small bag of clothes at my feet. "What happened to you?" she nodded toward my arms.

She watched intently as I recounted my story, nodding, raising her eyebrows, and offering the guttural "mmhmm," as Rwandans often do to show acknowledgment or agreement. When I finished, she paused, taking it all in.

After a moment she offered, "There's an American woman, Madame Carr, who runs an orphanage here in Gisenyi. You could probably sleep there." I thanked her for the bread and her directions and went on my way, finding the Imbabazi Orphanage just as she had described it.

Rosamond Carr had originally opened the orphanage in

1994 to take in children displaced by the genocide. She had moved to Rwanda in 1949, and later, against all social norms, she bought and managed a pyrethrum plantation near the Virunga Mountains. In 1994, the genocide forced her to leave her home. When she returned a few months later, the plantation was in shambles and her people in great need. Together with her staff, at the age of eighty-two, she rehabilitated her home into an orphanage and became a family for the many children who found themselves without one.

Through the end of 1997 and early 1998, the same resurgence that had taken my hands threatened her home and her children. After gunfire continued to ring out around her farm, she packed up the children and moved the orphanage to a church-owned building in Gisenyi.

It was there that I asked for the infamous Madame Carr.

"She's gone for the night. Come back in the morning," the cook told me by the back door.

The next morning, when Madame Carr arrived, I was waiting by the front door. She eyed me warily but compassionately as I repeated my story and understated my need. "I just need a place to stay while I look for work."

"Wait here," she told me and reappeared a few minutes later with an older gentleman.

Together we rode to Abadahogora, a center for street boys near the orphanage. Madame Carr sat with me as the center director asked me a barrage of questions.

"Do you smoke?"

"No."

"Have you ever stolen anything?"

"*No.*"

"Everyone here takes care of himself. How will *you* take care of yourself?"

I had no reply. I honestly didn't know. But how could I take care of myself if I was never given the chance?

"Look, maybe the Catholic center can help him," the director offered, and together Madame Carr and I went to request their help.

"I'm sorry, madame. We only help with clothes, things like that. We have no place to care for him or even for him to sleep."

My heart sank yet again. I should have never left home. I had barely eaten in days and at this point wouldn't even have the strength to make the daylong walk back to Ramba. I had nowhere to go.

Madame Carr again thanked the sister cordially and instructed the driver to take us back to the Imbabazi. Once there, she sat me down and looked me over, as if searching for answers. I knew she was just delaying the inevitable—another impossible search for a place to belong.

"Frederick, I'm not sure how we can help you, but for now, you can stay here."

I couldn't believe it. I thanked her for the kindness that no one else had shown, and she sent me off with one of the teachers to show me around.

I later learned that as soon as I left her office, she picked up the phone and dialed the United States.

"Hello, Charlene?"

"Roz, is something wrong?"

"No, no, everything is fine. I just—well, a boy, Frederick, has just arrived, and I'm not sure what to do with him."

She recounted my story to Charlene Jendry, the director and cofounder of Columbus Zoo's Partners In Conservation. PIC was founded as a conservation organization in 1991 when Charlene, then a gorilla keeper, and some docents at the zoo wanted to reach beyond the gates of the zoo and help gorillas in their natural habitats. But in 1995, when Charlene received a letter from Madame Carr requesting financial help for the Imbabazi Orphanage, PIC added humanitarian efforts to their conservation organization. Through those efforts, they've learned that by taking care of the people, they are also taking care of the land that the animals call home.

Over the years, Madame Carr had come to confide in Charlene, especially where the children were concerned.

"You know, Charlene, he could be very worldly, and my little children are not worldly."

Charlene knew exactly what she meant. I was older than the other children at the orphanage. Street boys my age commonly resorted to less-than-honorable means to make ends meet and often picked up adult habits, such as smoking and drinking. Plus, seeing that my hands had been deliberately cut off, she knew that there was a possibility that my story was completely contrived. There were rumors of boys being dismembered and discharged from the Interahamwe's "army" after they had failed to follow orders. The genocide had made us all wary of our fellow man, even the young and disabled.

However, Madame Carr and Charlene were not as quick to dismiss me as the others had been.

"I think we will keep him one week," Roz finally told Charlene.

Of course, I didn't know anything about these discussions. I was just grateful for a place to stay. I tried to be the smallest burden and the biggest help possible. The teachers and even the children did all they could to teach me to help myself. When meals were served, I was given a spoon or fork just like everyone else. The kids would giggle when I—quite often—dropped the spoon and sent food flying, but they would also cheer when I finally manipulated one bean into my mouth. The kids welcomed me into their ball games and were amazed when I caught the ball in my arms or would even toss it to them. Their energy propelled me to try even harder.

I also found comfort in those new friendships. I quickly learned that many of the children, even those much younger than I was, had survived and witnessed horrible things. Some were found buried underneath dead bodies, and others had watched in hiding as their families were murdered. It helped to talk about it with them, and I knew if those little kids could survive and even find joy after something like that, I could too.

Only two days after their first discussion of me, Madame Carr called Charlene again. "I wanted to let you know that we are keeping Frederick."

Although I was older than the rest, I was quickly accepted as one of the children, the one big brother to a much larger family than the one I had left at home. Before too long I had almost mastered my basic care. I was provided clothes that could be pulled on and taken off relatively easily, with no buttons or zippers to complicate matters. I could bathe with soapy water, although handling the soap still proved quite impossible. Even though I was rather slow compared to someone with hands, I was feeling more independent than ever.

It became a game, a never-ending challenge. What else could I do with my arms? What could I do that everyone else *knew* I couldn't? What would everyone say is impossible for me?

If I can eat with a spoon, I reasoned, *maybe I can also write with a pencil.*

So when I found a pencil and paper lying on the meeting room table, I decided to give it a shot. I laid my left arm on the table to the left of the pencil, and with the end of my right arm, I tried to roll the pencil onto the end of my left arm. It took several attempts, but before long I was holding the pencil between the ends of my arms. After a while, I was able to position the pencil at an angle that was conducive for writing, and slowly, carefully, I wrote my name.

Not bad, I thought, and I began to try to draw.

Soon after, Madame Carr walked in and saw me holding the pencil. She looked at the butterfly perched atop a flower I had drawn on the page. "Frederick! Why, that's—that's amazing! That's beautiful!" And she ran out of the room.

Puzzled, I dropped the pencil and stared at the doorway.

Within moments she was back with a notebook in hand. "Here! This is for you. Keep drawing! When you run out of paper, I'll get you more!"

And I did. I drew and drew and drew. I sketched animals and birds, people and plants. I couldn't stop drawing. I knew then that I wanted to be an artist, but even more than that, I knew then that I *could*.

Not long into my stay there, Madame Carr called me into her office, the orphanage's storeroom that also held her desk and some chairs.

"Frederick, I'd like you to meet Charlene and Bobby Jendry and Jeff Ramsey. They're visiting from the United States."

I grinned from ear to ear and gave each of them a huge hug. Charlene laughed, taken aback. Madame Carr explained about PIC, and before I knew it, we were all talking about the possibility of getting new hands, prosthetics that could help me to do even more than I was doing now.

"This will take time," Charlene told me, "but we will see what we can do."

Just the thought of it was more than I could imagine. What would they look like? What would they feel like? How would I use them and move them? How long would I have to wait? What else could I do with hands?! These were all answers that couldn't come soon enough. But I would have plenty to keep me busy while I waited.

Madame Carr soon announced that the Imbabazi Orphanage would be moving to a new location. Our lease was up with the church, and she and Mr. Sembagare, who helped run the orphanage, had found a larger place to move.

Charlene, along with some other members of the PIC team, came to help the staff prepare for the move, and I was eager to do whatever I could to help. It was a lot of work, but it was also a lot of fun. We would sing songs as we worked, and neighborhood kids would watch through the windows, amazed at seeing the *abazungu* (white people) hard at work.

In the small villages, high in the hills, we never saw white people at all. In fact, when we were little, we were told that white people would use our heads for alligator bait. So we didn't *want* to see any white people. But here in Gisenyi, the white people were usually tourists, riding in cars or relaxing out on the shore of Lake Kivu. Sweating, scrubbing white people were quite a sight for these Rwandan children!

Being all too aware of my newfound love for painting, Madame Carr assigned me the task of painting the bunk beds. I couldn't believe it: the boy with no hands, *painting the beds*. It was truly a dream come true. I sang softly as I carefully dipped the brush into the bright-blue paint.

"*Muraho*," a voice called.

I looked up from my paintbrush.

"*Amakuru?*" a tall young man asked. "How are you?"

"*Ni meza*," I answered, wondering how I hadn't seen him before.

"*Nitwa* Zacharie. *Witwande?*" he asked me, tilting his head as he looked at the brush in my arms.

"*Nitwa* Frederick." I smiled.

And that was how I met Zacharie Dusingizimana. He had already introduced himself to Madame Carr and Charlene, offering his help in cleaning up the new center and with translations between the English-speaking PIC team and the Kinyarwanda-speaking locals. I had no idea then, but what began as a simple introduction would develop into one of the most meaningful friendships and partnerships of my life.

nine

beautiful fingers

*"It's pretty difficult to go back to your little
everyday troubles after meeting him."*
—Jason Macedonia, Hanger Prosthetics

After that first day when Zacharie showed up to help, he never really left.

He helped us clean everything up and settle in to our new location. Then he stayed around to read books to us in English. Even though the books were meant for primary school kids, I was eager to learn more of the English language, however it was made available to me. Soon Madame Carr was able to create a position for Zacharie and hire him as a full-time English teacher. I'm not sure who was more excited about his being there—Zacharie or us children.

Each day followed a regular, but not regimented, routine at the Imbabazi Orphanage, waking up around six thirty for breakfast so that those going to public school would be ready in time. The preschoolers spent the morning with Madame

Carr, while I went for English with Zacharie. I would sit in on the regular English class; plus he would have an extra lesson for me to complete on my own. The afternoons held other classes, but also drawing, painting, and writing thank-you cards to donors who supported the orphanage. Dinner was served around six o'clock in the evening, and bedtime came at eight thirty. Between classes, we'd often play cards or have soccer games. Then at night, we'd entertain each other with stories before bed.

Because I was older, I was occasionally allowed to venture out into town for errands. Sometimes if I was going far, and sometimes just for fun, I would take the old bicycle that I had taught myself to ride at the orphanage. I think it made Madame Carr a bit nervous, but after a while, I could ride that bike just as well as a boy with two hands.

On one trip, I passed a familiar face on the street and screeched to a halt. It was her—one of the girls who had saved me that night!

I laid my bike down right there in the street and ran up to her. "Do you remember me?"

"Yes, yes!" she said, shaking her head in shock.

I jumped into a hug. "I don't think I ever asked your name," I said when I let her go.

"Claudine. Claudine Umeza. And I know that you are Frederick," she said. "My sister's husband had a relative in the hospital at the same time you were there. He told us that you were okay, but I never dreamed . . ."

"Yes, things are good." I nodded proudly. "I'm staying at the

Imbabazi Orphanage here in Gisenyi. I'm learning to take care of myself and even doing some drawing—"

"And riding a bicycle!"

"Yes," I said. "Because of you. Thank you."

"God is good." She smiled. "Thank you for stopping me, for letting me know you're okay. *More* than okay."

After a moment, we said our good-byes, and I gave her one last hug. I jumped back on my bicycle and rode back into the life that she—with a little divine guidance—had made possible.

I continued to work on my drawing at the orphanage, eventually branching off into painting. Madame Carr always saw to it that I had whatever materials I needed, although I'm not sure where she found them. I didn't remember ever seeing acrylics or watercolors or even the little paintbrushes at the market, but she was always able to find them, announcing to me when she had returned with a fresh supply.

The kids would often sit and watch me as long as time allowed, and I'd try to draw or paint whatever they requested. They were amazed—as was I—that a boy with no hands had such control, could create such beauty, without hands or fingers to manipulate the tools of an artist.

We also were given the opportunity to explore the art of photography through a special project, "Through the Eyes of Children," conceived by a professional photographer, David Jiranek (whom I would later visit in New York). He and his crew came from the United States to our orphanage in Rwanda and explained the project to us. They showed us these cameras made out of paper and plastic—"disposable" cameras, we were told.

They gave one to each of us, showed us how the cameras worked, and gave us a lesson in photography. They gave us some time over the next few days to collect our images and encouraged us to take photos of things that we found interesting.

There were a limited number of exposures on that camera, so I selected my subjects carefully. Balancing the camera along the length of my left arm, I steadied it with my right arm and looked through, holding my subjects in the small, black view-finder as steadily as I could before pressing the button with the end of my right arm. I captured images of people passing on the road and the scene at the meat market, one at a beauty salon, one of a boy selling cabbages. When the exposures were spent, I turned in my camera, and like magic, the pictures of what I had seen came back to me on paper.

Madame Carr proudly displayed our photographs along the walls of the orphanage, creating our own little art gallery there. David's team also helped to arrange the photos in albums so that we could hold them in our arms and look at them again and again. David and his team were so proud of what we had done, and before we knew it, people all the way in the United States knew about our little project. Photos from our orphanage were regularly featured in exhibits honoring Rwandan culture, including at the US Embassy in Kigali, at one of President Paul Kagame's talks, and even at a launch of the American film *Hotel Rwanda*.

David Jiranek died in 2003, but not before his passion for photography had changed the lives and perspectives of a group of kids in Rwanda and beyond. By entrusting innocent, unassuming eyes to capture the world around them, he provided the outside world with a pure, unique perspective of the everyday lives of post-genocide Rwandans. This idea, born from a passion for his work and the people he encountered, grew into a beautiful international representation of the rebirth and rebuilding of our country.

As I had been learning English and exploring my artistic abilities, the Columbus Zoo had been making the arrangements for the trip that would forever change my life; they would fly me to the United States and see to it that I was furnished with new hands. I'll probably never know all of the pieces and parts they had to pull together to make it happen. But I know that the result was simply another miracle.

They worked with Madame Carr to get my visa paperwork filed and approved. They even found a doctor in Rwanda who would accompany me to the States and help translate while I was there. Jack Hanna's family doctor and longtime friend, Nick Baird, reached out to a Columbus hand surgeon, Dr. James Nappi, who in turn contacted Hanger Prosthetics there in Columbus to create the hands. After hearing my story, they agreed to furnish the hands and the related treatment at no charge.

I didn't know it at the time, but I had just been offered free hands by probably the most innovative prosthetics company in the United States, maybe even the world, a company founded by a man with whom I shared some similarities. The company's website tells how James E. Hanger gained the uncoveted title of the first amputee of the Civil War after a cannonball shattered his leg just a few days into battle. After some time as a prisoner of war, he returned home and asked to be left alone. His family assumed he was needing time to process the trauma, so it was quite a shock when he came walking down the stairs on his new leg that he had carved from the wood of a barrel as he lay in bed. That same year he began developing prosthetic limbs for others, and Hanger Prosthetics has been doing it ever since.

As the day approached for me to go get my new hands, I had no idea what to expect. I'd never been outside of our tiny country, except for that brief period in the Congo, much less to a whole different continent. Of course, I'd always heard stories about the legendary America, but nothing could prepare me for what I would find on the other side of the world.

I don't think I slept for days before my flight, and I don't think I touched the ground for my first days there in the States. Everything—absolutely everything—was so new and different. The language, the faces, the lights, the cars, the houses, the water, the food. Everything I saw was so completely unlike anything I'd ever seen or tasted or heard. Every one of my senses was in complete overload.

But I wasn't allowed any time to be overloaded. We had to get immediately to work. The prosthetics process usually takes months and even years to perfect, and I only had a few weeks in the States. We had to complete everything from the initial evaluation all the way to occupational therapy in that timeframe. Fortunately for me, I was in excellent hands; PIC and the Hanger team had thought of every last detail. And then some.

Jack Hanna, then the director of the Columbus Zoo, had been traveling to Rwanda for years, filming for his television shows. He had fallen in love with the country and was a huge supporter of PIC's projects there. When he heard about me, he got in touch with Charlie Gibson, an anchor on ABC's *Primetime*, to tell him my story.

After I arrived in the States, a crew showed up to film my visit and document the entire process. I was staying with Charlene and Bobby Jendry, and the camera crews were always there, recording us as we rode in the car, at home in the evenings, and as we met with the doctors and staff at Hanger. They were all really thoughtful and helpful, but proved to be another overwhelming element of the American life.

The six-hour time difference from Rwanda to Columbus was confusing in itself. Then the crews, in trying to create certain backdrops and effects, would set the rooms in Charlene's house to look like day or night, depending on the scene. I would walk from my bedroom at night to find the dining room lit up like daytime. At another time, they wanted to film me getting ready for bed, but it was the middle of the day.

I went to Charlene. "They want me to pray, but we usually pray together at night. What do we do?"

She smiled at me. "It's only for the movie, Frederick. Just do whatever you're comfortable with."

As odd as the request was, the crew was really helpful and understanding. I knew they were only trying to share my story, to maybe inspire people all over the world. So there, in the middle of the day, I got ready for bed and said my prayers with Charlene.

That night—when it was *really* nighttime—after we had said our prayers again, I asked Charlene, "How long are we going to be making this movie?"

And then there was that one-on-one interview with Mr. Gibson, to talk about how I lost my hands. As we talked, I began to recount the moments that had brought me here: the bus ride, the electrical cords, the pain of losing my hands, the recovery. And I knew that before long, people all over the United States—and beyond—would know my story, how God had brought a young Rwandan boy around the world to give him new hands.

From the moment I stepped off the plane, every second had been a thrill, every moment a new experience. But at no time was I more excited than when in the lab at Hanger, watching them create my new hands.

Back in Rwanda, Madame Carr and Charlene had helped me learn about the different options that were available, so that I would know what to expect. Some prosthetic hands looked like real hands, but they were really only aesthetic, lacking the functionality of the more hook-like instruments. I knew that the priority definitely was something functional. I wasn't really worried about how my hands looked; I guess I had finally gotten past that. More than anything, I wanted my hands to work. I wanted to be able to zip a zipper, to tie my shoes by myself. Still, with the hooks, there wasn't an option that had five fingers; I wasn't so sure that having only two silver fingers would help me at all.

Being half a world away from Hanger, I also needed something that I could easily maintain and repair by myself with supplies I could find at home, far from the precise power tools

Frederick on I Am Able bike tour

Zacharie and Frederick at the UCC

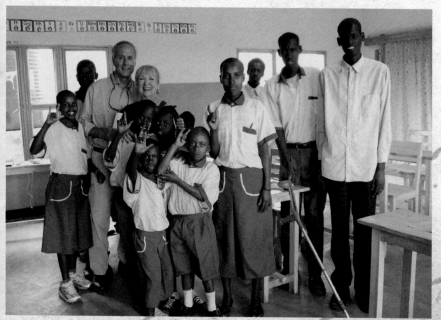

Jack Hanna and Charlene Jendry with students at the UCC

Amy Parker

The bridge where the men ambushed Frederick's bus;
their camp was located on the hill in the distance.

Amy Parker

The home of the two sisters, where Frederick
stayed the night after he lost his arms

Jack Hanna

Frederick and Zacharie with Jack and Suzi Hanna

Amy Parker

Frederick, his mother, and youngest brother

Amy Parker

Looking down from Frederick's
childhood home (where his
mother still lives today)

Christie Abel

Frederick and Christie after
completing the first I Am Able ride

Amy Parker

The platform where Frederick spent
most of his year at the Gisenyi Hospital

Amy Parker

The main house at the
Imbabazi Orphanage

Amy Parker

One of the mass graves at the
Kigali Memorial Centre

Jack Hanna

Frederick and Jack Hanna at the UCC

Amy Parker

Amy Parker

The tall eucalyptus trees of Rwanda   The cook at the Gisenyi Hospital

Amy Parker

The current kitchen at the Gisenyi Hospital

Christie Abel

The I Am Able team, gathering before the ride

Christie Abel

Frederick, climbing a hill during the ride

Christie Abel

Frederick, greeting the crowds on the first I Am Able ride

Amy Parker

A student at the UCC

Amy Parker

UCC math class for deaf students

Amy Parker

UCC ladies hand-sewing dolls

Amy Parker

Banana-leaf crafting at the UCC

Amy Parker

Frederick overlooking the building
site of the UCC preschool

Jack Hanna

Classroom at the UCC

Amy Parker

Traditional Rwandan dancing
in Volcanoes National Park

Grahm S. Jones

Frederick speaking at the
Rwandan Fête in 2011

Frederick painting one of his beautiful landscapes

One of Frederick's paintings

here in the Hanger clinic. For me, this trip to the United States was a once-in-a-lifetime chance; I didn't know that I would ever be back again. These hands needed to last me a long time.

With all of the preliminary information in hand, the people at Hanger were briefed and ready for me when I arrived. They went well beyond absorbing the cost of the prostheses, which would typically be anywhere from twelve to twenty thousand US dollars. They also shut down their entire operation for the day to focus on me, to create my hands quickly with me there on site, to make sure the process went as smoothly and efficiently as possible. I had an entire team of caring experts waiting on me: doctors, occupational and physical therapists, the prosthetists—the men and women fitting and constructing the hands—and the clinic manager overseeing it all. They could have understandably had us sitting in the lobby throughout the process, during regular business hours, waiting our turn with the other patients, and we would have been happy to do so, but they did absolutely everything imaginable to ensure that my first experience with prosthetics was a successful one.

There was continually someone attending to me. One person would take precise measurements of my arms, back, and shoulders. Another showed me the materials they would use to shape the socket, where the prosthesis would fit onto my arm. They created plaster molds of my arms to get the exact contours; they fitted me with a cloth sleeve that would protect my skin and allow the hands to fit more snugly.

Once actually in Hanger's workshop, they demonstrated and explained every step of the production process to me.

Charlene remarked that it was like "Santa's workshop" in there—every person doing a unique job, eight or nine people each handcrafting a different part of my new hands. They sewed the suspenders-like harness from scratch and shaped the socket perfectly to fit the plaster mold of my arms. They invited me to watch as they worked, educating me about what each part did and how to adjust it. They encouraged me to touch and feel the tension of the wires and the pressure of the hooks so that I would know how to tell when they were adjusted properly. They explained how the harness would not only secure the arms but would also allow me to operate the hooks, opening and closing them with the muscles in my upper arms, shoulders, and back. By the time the hands were finished, I felt like I was just as much of an expert on prosthetic hands as Hanger was!

In that moment when they walked into the room with my finished hands, I wouldn't have been any happier if they had been crowning me king. Over the soft sleeves they slipped the durable, carbon-fiber cones with shiny silver hooks onto each arm. They adjusted the harness that wrapped around my back and shoulders and connected to the sockets.

The process of learning to function with new prostheses usually takes months—months we did not have—so they had a therapist there to work with me immediately, one-on-one. But once they slipped those hooks on my arms, it was as if they instantly became a part of me, as if I were born with the knowledge of how to use them. As soon as they had secured them on my body, the fingers went to work. I picked up a marker and began to write.

My eyes were as wide as my smile. The Hanger team seemed equally ecstatic, I assumed because of my new hands. But the truth was, they had never seen anyone with the ability to control the hooks as quickly as I did. It was unheard of—they stood silently in tearful awe as those silver hooks came to life.

The *Primetime* crew was filming throughout the whole process, as the hands were formed, as I picked up the marker, during my occupational therapy sessions.

When the therapist asked what I wanted to do with my hands, I told her, "I want to build a house." And I wasn't kidding. I had dreamed of having my own home one day, and I knew in order to do so, I would probably have to build it myself.

"Well," she said with a laugh, "I guess I need to show you how to use a hammer!"

She left and quickly reappeared with a hammer, wood, and nails, and she patiently guided me in adjusting the tension and positioning my fingers to hammer a nail. I was surprised at how easy it was, how smoothly the fingers responded to my commands.

When we got into the car, I couldn't wait until we got back to Charlene's house. As soon as we did, I said, "I'll be back!" and ran to my room. Carrying my lace-up shoes, I ran back past Charlene and out to the patio. I sat on that patio for hours, determined to make those silver hooks create a knotted bow.

"Look! Look! I did it!" I called, dancing.

Charlene came out to the patio beaming. She knew how important it was for me to dress myself—lace-up shoes and all.

She continued challenging me at home, filling a basket with items of different sizes and textures. I would pick them up, handle them, and place them back. As I mastered all of the items in the basket, Charlene would find new things, more difficult things for me to pick up and handle, but by the second night, I had her stumped: I was able to pick up a straight pin with my new fingers.

Even from the first mention of the new hands, I was warned that prosthetic hands would not be like my old hands, that they would be tools, not replacements for human hands. The doctors and therapists had prepared me, saying that I would reach points of discouragement and that I should be patient and work through those. But it never happened. I refused to let it.

In one quiet moment when Charlene and I were alone, away from the cameras, she asked me, "Well, Frederick, what do you think about your new hands?"

I looked at the hooks and said, "These are not hands." I took in a deep breath. "These are beautiful fingers."

The trip back to Rwanda felt like the longest ride ever. I could not wait to show everyone at the orphanage my new hands.

I was welcomed home like a hero. All of the kids and staff kids gathered around me, cheering and crowding in to try to get a look at my new fingers. I was exhausted but eagerly obliged.

Then they pelted me with questions.

"What was it like in America?"

"Was it just like heaven?"

"Why did you come back?"

I told them about all of the lights, the people, and the very tall houses. I told them there were as many cars as spoons in their houses—*everybody* had one. I told them that, yes, it was true: they had *everything* there.

"But," I said in all sincerity, "this is home."

As the days passed, I tried my new fingers on all of my old routines. The tiny points held a zipper nicely. At mealtime, I entertained the kids by showing them how well the rubber grips held a spoon. The new fingers offered a new level of independence that I had been hoping for.

But when I returned to painting, the fingers, well, they felt awkward. As easy as it was to adjust to all of the other tasks, painting just felt more natural without my hands. I could feel the weight of the paint on the brush, the wood of the handle against my skin, and the texture of the canvas or paper as I wiped the color across to give birth to a scene. I experimented with the colors, recreating sweeping African sunsets or traditional Rwandan homes graced by tall slender women elongated by the clay jugs on their heads. And after a while, it was clear that painting without my hands was the only way that made sense.

Granted, I loved my new fingers. I had traveled across the world to get them and the independence that they promised. But I also realized that my God-given ability to create something beautiful had been there all along.

ten

faith and forgiveness

"The fact that today, I have my new fingers, I can give testimony that there are good people in the world. Because of that, I can forget what happened to me in 1998."

—FREDERICK

There was no way to fully express the gratitude I felt toward Madame Carr and Charlene Jendry for my new footing in life. But I also knew that if I were going to be truly independent, I couldn't get too comfortable at the orphanage.

Besides, I wasn't exactly a child anymore. My best friend there at the orphanage was Zacharie, the English teacher. He was so encouraging, so patient with all of my questions and struggles with learning the complicated language that our conversations often veered off in many other directions. He and I spent day after day talking about what life would be like after the orphanage, and he would listen and offer guidance for my many concerns and plans for the future. I could always make him laugh, and although he wasn't much older than I was, he would always be ready with a wise word when I needed it.

Within a few months' time, I had secured a job delivering fabric to sellers in the market. It would provide enough income for me to afford rent for a small house. It was very basic—two rooms with no running water or electricity—but more than enough for me. I would walk to the Congo in the mornings and buy the fabric at a wholesale price, then carry it to different markets in Gisenyi to sell for a small profit. I would go to four or five markets each day, mostly walking, but sometimes I took a taxi when I needed to go farther out. The buyers in the market were helpful and kind, and it hardly seemed like work talking to the buyers and the other shoppers all day. But the best part was that it provided an income—enough for me to make it on my own.

A week didn't pass, however, without going back to visit the orphanage, now a seven-minute walk from my house. I would mainly stop in to talk with Zacharie, but I always checked in with Madame Carr and the children to let them know how I was doing, to see how they were making it without me there to entertain them.

I gained other friends around town too. I had my regular customers at the market and spent the day chatting with the sellers near me. Through the market, I had gotten to know one of the sisters at the local Catholic church as well. She would often meet me for coffee in the mornings before the day got underway.

One particular morning, she and I were talking about matters of faith, when a man approached the counter. He ordered his drink and turned to see me sitting there.

"Hey, I know you."

I looked around.

"I know who you are."

My friend turned to the man then back to me, awaiting my reply.

I wasn't sure who the man was, but I certainly had an idea. "I'm sorry." I focused on my coffee. "You must have me confused with someone else."

"You're grown up now, but I'm sure it was you." He came closer.

Of course, it was difficult to hide my lack of hands, but I was shocked. I was afraid. I searched for courage and strength.

Finally, I looked up at him. "Okay, how do you know me?"

"When you were younger, our men brought you to us." He spoke softly but without hesitation. "We cut off your hands."

I didn't answer.

"I was the one who took all of your clothes."

Then I found my voice. "Yes. That was me," I began. And out came an uncontrollable flood of all of the memories of that day. I reminded that man of every detail of every heinous act that he and his men had committed—killing the men, raping the women, and just watching as they cut off my arms and left me for dead. I spared him no detail of what I had experienced that day, of what I had carried around every day since.

He looked as if he might take off running.

I reached up, laid my arm on his, and looked directly into his eyes. "But I already forgive you."

His eyes grew wide as he searched for a reply.

But I didn't wait for it. I was uncomfortably hot and could sit no longer. I said good-bye and walked out into the street.

My sister friend trailed behind me. "Frederick, wait! Are you okay? How—why would that man even say that to you?"

I stopped and turned to her. "I'm fine. Really I am."

In fact, at that moment, I was so much better than fine. A huge weight had been lifted from me, a weight I had been carrying so long. Even with new fingers and a new life, I hadn't been able to escape the hatred that held me trapped in the memories of that day. Although that man had frightened me briefly, he had also forever freed me.

No. I had freed myself.

I chose the best of the fabrics from that morning's supply and tucked it away for later. Then early the next morning, I packed the fabric in a bag, put on my lace-up shoes, and headed home to the hills of Ramba.

A bus from Gisenyi carried me to Ngororero, and from there I would walk the remaining distance, about an hour and a half at a normal pace. As I walked the paths that led to home, I appreciated them like never before. While passing the homes in the villages, I noted how every single centimeter of their yards was put to work for them, how avocado trees hung above coffee beans and banana trees swung above pineapple plants to make the most efficient use of land. I took joy in every child who waved as I went by, and I wished a hearty *"Muraho!"* to the tireless women carrying baskets on their heads, children on their backs, and pulling a goat or two behind them.

I passed a group of men and skirted women, working side by side with shovels and pickaxes to clear a landslide that was blocking the road. It was probably these same men and women, and dozens of others like them, who had laid each of the thousands of stones that comprised the ditches along the road.

I took pride in the graduated terraces that measured off the mountains in neatly laid rows, knowing that each and every one of them was cut into the earth with hoes and picks swung by Rwandan hands. I surveyed the vast fields of tea and coffee beans that seemed to cover every inch of the surrounding hills. Almost tasting the sweet reward they would yield, I was struck anew by the ingenuity of the beehives that seemed to be randomly hoisted in the trees along the road. I noted how the bright green of the mountains seemed to deepen into a midnight blue in the distance.

Breathing in the minty smell of eucalyptus, I admired their rusty trunks and was grateful for their thirsty roots that drank the water from the soil before it could erode away the land. Waving to the men making charcoal below, I valued their thankless labor and knew the warmth it would bring. I let the wind wrap around me and carry me higher as I reached the tops of the hills, and I soaked in the warm African sun as I almost ran downhill into the valleys. After climbing and descending about five of those notorious Rwandan hills, I could finally see the hill that I called home.

My brothers and sisters spotted me before I reached the top. They ran down the path and circled around me. "Frederick's here! Look, Mum, look!" they called to her from below.

When I reached the house, my mother was waiting there, teary-eyed. I picked her up in a hug, and she laughed and tisked, adjusting her tightly wrapped headdress that I'd knocked askew.

"This is for you." I proudly handed her the fabric. She ran her hand across the brightly colored pattern and held it to her chest.

It was good to be home, together again.

We sat down, and I asked my mother how everything had been. I told her all about Madame Carr and the Imbabazi Orphanage, about the trip to the United States, and the man in the coffee shop. She listened with a faint smile as I went on and on about my little house and Zacharie and my days in the market.

"I was so worried about you," she said when I paused.

"I know," I said, then plainly stated what I had been trying to tell her all along. "I'm doing good, Mum. I'm going to be okay."

But I think she already knew.

eleven

why did i survive?

"Your sacrifices are a gift to the nation. They are the seed from which the new Rwanda grows."
—Rwandan President Paul Kagame

Back in Gisenyi, I found Charlene and others from the Columbus Zoo's PIC team visiting the orphanage. Charlene and I spent the afternoon catching up, and I told her all about my new home, my newfound independence.

As the sun faded and a calm quiet hushed over the city, we sat for a few moments in pensive silence.

"Charlene," I asked, still looking into the night, "why do you think I survived?"

She looked at me and thought for a moment. "Frederick, why do *you* think you survived?"

Without hesitation, I answered, "I think God wants me to help people like me."

She smiled with a slow nod. "I think you may be right."

It was constantly on my mind. As I walked to the Congo

to pick up the fabric each morning, while I was standing in the market, when I lay in bed at night, I was always thinking about how I could do it. How could I help people like me?

I had very little money. It wasn't like I could build a home for them or even donate to half of the beggars I passed on the street. But there was a feeling I could not shake. I had to do something.

"Zacharie, what do you think we can do for them? For the street children and the ones like me?"

"What do you mean?"

"I don't know, like a place where we could all come together, where everyone would feel at home."

"A school where we could teach them English." He grinned.

"Yes, yes! And feed them."

"And train them for work."

"Provide clothes and soap . . ."

We both mulled the idea, all too aware of our limited resources.

"What about playing ball?" he offered.

"Ball?"

"Yes. It's something we could do right now, with what we have."

"Okay." That made sense. Zacharie always made sense. "What kind of ball?"

"I don't know. Volleyball?"

I laughed. Me, with no hands, playing volleyball?

But God has a way of proving Himself to those who laugh at His ideas. The next thing I knew, there were two teams of beggars and disabled people playing volleyball in the churchyard.

And I was the coach.

The sisters would sometimes watch, tolerating us at first with a wary eye, but with time, they almost seemed to enjoy our being there. Zacharie usually sat off to the side with a knowing smile. He would cheer and clap, but he made sure that we were always the stars of the game.

After awhile, though, we knew. This wasn't enough. We could do more.

"We could teach them," Zacharie suggested. "We could teach them English."

"Of course!" I agreed.

So there in the churchyard, we added English lessons around our volleyball games.

We told everyone about what we were doing, spreading the word, looking for ways to expand our little mission. The need was so great; it seemed that everywhere I turned there was a man sitting in the dirt on withered legs or an aimless young girl with half-closed milky eyes. It physically hurt me to see them there; I had once felt their despair and found my way out. I had to find a way to lead them out too.

***

I had just entered Gisenyi with a load of fabric when I heard my name.

"Frederick!"

"There he is!"

"Frederick, Frederick, a lady is looking for you!" The child danced as he called to me.

I looked across the road to see Zacharie coming toward me with a group of kids from the orphanage.

"What are they talking about?" I asked him.

"It's true. There is an American lady at the orphanage asking for you. She wants to meet you."

"Charlene? Someone from PIC?"

He shook his head. "It's a Jessica McCall. From California?"

I was baffled. I knew no one named Jessica and certainly no one from California. But when I later met her, she knew exactly who I was.

"I saw your story on *Primetime*," she explained immediately. She saw my brow furrow.

"On television, in America, with Charlie Gibson," she explained. "I came to meet Ms. Carr, to visit the orphanage, but I wanted to meet you too."

She wanted to know more about my story and what I was doing now, since the segment had aired. She listened intently as I told her a little bit about my job, my painting, my volleyball coaching. But I told her that I wanted to do more, that I wanted to help people like me.

I took her to meet my friends at a volleyball game to show her the need, the potential to do more. And later, as she talked with Zacharie and me, we discussed the possibility of opening a center to help the disabled and disadvantaged in Gisenyi.

"We could probably use a classroom at the church," Zacharie offered.

"Zacharie could teach English, and I could teach painting." I added.

Jessica nodded. "And I'll help with desks and chairs and whatever supplies you need."

Zacharie and I looked at each other in disbelief.

"You know," I said to Jessica, "we've been praying for someone like you. We knew what we wanted to do, but we needed someone to help us."

A center for people like me, right here in Gisenyi, would be a dream come true for us all. Jessica had come to Rwanda with a load of teddy bears for the orphans of Gisenyi—seeking out the poorest of the poor, searching for a way to make a difference. And Zacharie and I had done what we could, but we wanted to make a bigger impact right here in our neighborhood, helping others like me. Working together, we could each give of what we had to make the others' dreams come true.

Zacharie and I sat in the churchyard sipping cold Fantas after a game.

He tilted his head toward the buildings. "Maybe they have a room or something we could use."

"Let's ask them!"

The priest looked at me, then back to Zacharie. "Let me understand this. You two . . . are going to teach classes . . . to disabled people? People off the streets?"

"Yes sir!" I nodded.

He turned to the enthusiastic nodding. "And *you're* going to teach *painting?*"

"Yes sir." I couldn't keep from smiling.

"Well, okay." He chuckled, shaking his head. "If you think you can pull it off, come on."

"So, yes? We can use the room?" Zacharie confirmed.

"Yes, yes, you can use the room."

We were beyond thrilled. We had a room! This was a real thing we were doing. My purpose had been fulfilled; my dream had come true.

But deep down, we knew: we were only getting started.

The room was already in pretty good shape, but Zacharie and I couldn't resist cleaning it and getting it ready for the first class. It took awhile for that first meeting to settle down; everyone was full of questions, wanting to know how we had gotten a classroom, how long we could meet there. We had tables and chairs, and for some of them, it was the closest they'd ever been to a real classroom.

Over the next few weeks, our borrowed room full of misfits even started to feel like a real classroom. We had set meeting times and salvaged school supplies. And we had a handful of very eager students. It was remarkable to see their progress week after week; it was obvious that they would never take for granted the opportunity to learn.

Yes, this was only the beginning.

twelve

building a dream

"Education is the only path to sustained peace."
—Ubumwe Community Center

As the excitement grew, the word about our classes
spread around Gisenyi-town. Of course, having Jack Hanna
there helped to stir things up a bit.

If a camera crew ever came to Rwanda, it was usually to
film the endangered mountain gorillas high in the Virunga
Mountains or maybe to see the variety of African wildlife on the
other side of the country at Akagera National Park. And occasionally, there were still some from the international media to
recount what had happened in the genocide, especially for the
previous year's ten-year anniversary.

However, I'm fairly confident that they had never been
here to film a menagerie of disabilities in a makeshift classroom. But Jack isn't one to do what's *usually* done, so when he
heard about our project—by way of Charlene—he threw his

full support behind it and brought his film crew to catch a volleyball game and to see our classroom in action.

After that—even more than already—it seemed that everyone wanted to see the English teacher and the man with no hands teaching their classroom of outliers. Our number of students started to grow, and soon that one room started to feel very, very small.

Then the priest approached us one day. "I'm sorry, gentlemen, but we're going to need that room from now on. Is there somewhere else you can go?"

"Yes, yes, we'll find something," Zacharie said calmly. "Thank you, Father."

What? How could that be?! I saw my dream completely crumble to the ground before the priest was even out of sight. The truth was, we had nothing. We knew we didn't have enough money to rent a room, and even if we did, it would be outgrown as soon as we got there. Jessica was still helping with supplies, and we simply couldn't ask her for anything else. Where would we go?

"What about PIC?" Zacharie suggested later. "They help the orphanage. They may be able to help us too."

"Sure," I agreed. Although I wasn't.

Yet in just a few days, we had word from PIC that, yes, they would indeed help with the rent on another place. We knew we had to tell Jessica about the move either way, and when we did, she insisted on helping to rent a new space as well. Before we knew it, in the way that only God provides, we had a two-room building full of people painting and practicing English. But most of all, it was a place where those who had been discarded by society could come together, find community, and in even the smallest of ways, begin slowly to improve their lives.

In 2006, about a year after his first visit, Jack Hanna and his crew came back, with Charlene, Jeff Ramsey, and other PIC members who were visiting Rwanda at the same time. They spent the afternoon with us in our new building in complete awe of the progress our project had made.

"Wow. This is just unbelievable." Jack raved over it all: the artwork displayed on the walls, the brief conversations the students carried in English, and even the sit-down volleyball games.

As he was leaving that evening, Jack pulled Charlene aside. "Charlene, after I leave, I want you to tell them that we're going to build them a school."

"But, Jack, we don't have the money to do that!"

"I'll figure that out," he said matter-of-factly. "I want you to tell them while you're here so they can start to look for land."

Charlene was incredulous. But at the same time, she had seen Jack in action before. When the Imbabazi Orphanage had reached out to PIC for funding, Charlene presented the request to Jack. Without hesitation, he said, "Tell her we'll cover her operating expenses." And somehow, they did.

So having no idea how it would happen, but knowing that it would, Charlene sat Zacharie and me down after everyone had left. She focused on the ground, gathering her thoughts before she spoke.

"Frederick, when you first told me about helping other disabled people, I thought it was a wonderful dream." She looked at me with a wry smile. "I thought it was *impossible*, but a wonderful dream."

I laughed, then saw the tears welling up in her eyes.

"What you and Zacharie have done here is beyond anything any of us could have imagined."

"Thank you," we answered, in soft unison.

"And we're going to help you do more." She leaned in and continued, "Jack wanted me to tell you that we're going to build you a school."

We sat motionless in stunned silence.

He was the first to recover. "A school?"

"Yes, your own place where you'll have plenty of room and . . ." She looked to me. "Everything you'll need to help people like you."

We couldn't believe it. We were completely blown away by how God had blessed our efforts. Nevertheless, we didn't want to waste a second in bringing this to a reality.

In a foggy state of disbelief, we immediately began examining our options. My experience in purchasing land was nonexistent; it was an idea only entertained in my most outrageous dreams. But if we had learned anything about this venture thus far, it was that we would need not only enough space for a building, but land with room to grow. It would need to be centrally located, in Gisenyi, easily accessible to the greatest number of people, especially those with difficulty walking and lacking funds for taxi transport. But in order for it to be affordable, it would need to be far enough away from the touristy shores of Lake Kivu on Gisenyi's western border. It took a whole year to find a parcel of land that was available and that met those requirements, but in 2007, PIC and the Columbus Zoo purchased a piece of Rwanda where our dreams would soon take shape.

In a planning meeting, Jack told Charlene, "I want it to be functional, but it has to look good too. The environment needs to communicate how much we value the people who are going to be in it. These people deserve that." With that, Jack firmly set in place the vision that we all had in our hearts.

Choosing a word that means "unity," we named it the Ubumwe Community Center (UCC). As building plans were being drawn and implemented, Zacharie and I were also creating plans for the ongoing programs within the center. We wanted to continue teaching English and art, but we knew that this was so much bigger. Our main mission was to provide educational, vocational, and basic life skills to people with disabilities so that they could learn to be self-reliant, and as a result gain self-esteem. After surveying the needs in our area, we created a multidimensional approach toward that goal, in a way that would make the center as impactful and inclusive as possible with the resources available to us. We would include both children and adults of varying degrees of ability, and ideally, we would reach far beyond the borders of our new property.

We laid out nine different programs: a classroom for mentally challenged children, inclusive education, work skills, computer skills, sign language, sports, home visits, wheelchair distribution, and Moving into Action. Our mentally challenged children would have a classroom of their own, where a skilled and understanding teacher would assist each student to learn on his level, from motor skill development to numbers and letters, even drawing and crafts.

Our inclusive education program was one of the first of its kind in our country. Despite the social stigma, we knew that physical disabilities had no effect on mental aptitude, that a person with one arm was just as intelligent as someone with two. We knew that a deaf person, when accommodated, was just as able to learn and eager to communicate as one who could hear. However, the existing schools simply didn't have the capacity to provide the extra assistance needed to integrate those children into mainstream classrooms. So the UCC would bridge the gap. We would provide the physical assistance—a bus ride to school, a wheelchair for mobility—and the mainstream classroom would provide the education. We would also have a teacher dedicated to our deaf students, teaching them sign language here at the center and providing interpretation when integrated into the mainstream schools. Together with the schools of Rwanda, we would see to it that physical handicaps no longer impeded a student's ability to learn.

Mainly for the older children and adults, we developed a Learning Center that would house several computer workstations, as well as a library that would be accessible to everyone. Gisenyi is unlike the rural areas in that most people have access to electricity; however, even in the large towns, few have the means or the need to purchase a computer. For that reason, we knew that proficiency or even a basic working knowledge in common computer programs—even knowing how to operate a mouse and a Start menu—would give them an advantage in the workforce. We also knew that a desk job would be the ideal employment for those whose physical disabilities made it difficult to walk or stand. The Learning Center would be a pinnacle of our program, making it at least equal to, if not more advanced than, the mainstream schools at the time.

In addition to computer, we would also have crafting classes for adults that could be used either to gain employment, to create goods for retail sale, or simply to be able to create affordable clothing and other items useful in the home. A tailor would teach students how to use a sewing machine, as well as make uniforms for the children. Some of the ladies would teach hand sewing through our doll-making classes. And as a simpler option for those who may not be able to sew, we would offer basket weaving and banana-leaf crafting activities. The crafts would be offered for sale at the market, with any proceeds going back into buying supplies and supporting the program as a whole.

We also knew that our program had to contain a wheelchair distribution element. That one simple tool could make an astounding difference for a child—or adult—who had been rendered immobile, for whatever reason. Without a wheelchair, a child would be left to sit in a dark house or out in the dirt all day. That physical positioning itself—alone, immobile, covered in dirt, with everyone looking down on him—would no doubt take a mental and emotional toll. Yet the benefits of a wheelchair were immeasurable. With it, the child would be lifted from the dirt and have access to an education and all of the opportunities beyond his front door. Making this part of our program would no doubt also present some challenges. One wheelchair would cost about four hundred US dollars, a year's salary for many Rwandans. And even if the funds were available, the wheelchairs usually were not. It could take months to find a wheelchair once the funds were in place. Still, we felt the wheelchair program would be worth every bit of the effort.

Of course, the sports program would offer fun and entertainment for everyone at the center. However, from a development standpoint, it would contribute benefits often neglected in programs that serve the physically challenged: motor skill development, hand-eye coordination, fitness, and team camaraderie, to name a few. By modifying games and creating teams based on the players' abilities, we could even the playing field and allow equal participation, offering everyone a chance to be active and competitive. Soccer, volleyball from a seated position, and even dancing—on knees and in wheelchairs—would allow most everyone to be a part of our sports program. Plus, learning to work together as a team would foster bonding and the development of group problem-solving skills. Most would come from an environment where there was no opportunity for any type of sports involvement.

Our home visits would focus on meeting basic needs for the disabled, but would also allow us to educate families about the services available to them. After the UCC received a referral of a disabled person unable to leave the home, a counselor would visit the home and assess the needs of the family. Ideally, this would result in allowing the disabled person to join the onsite UCC programs. This could simply happen through educating families, but the assessment could also indicate a need for a wheelchair or other assistance that would offer the person a means of transport to the center. However, in some cases, if the person were elderly, in general failing health, or otherwise bedbound, we would also provide for hygienic needs—such as delivering clothes or soap. These visits would typically be made on a monthly basis but also as the need arose.

But probably the most anticipated branch of the center was our Moving into Action program. The ultimate goal of the UCC would be the complete independence and integration of the disabled person into society. We would initiate the transition with job placement or on-the-job accommodation with the hope that our alumni would take what they had learned into the workplace and be able to subsist independently. As an alumnus moved into action, the benefits would reach far beyond that one disabled person; the program would benefit his entire family and maybe even see him move on to have a family of his own.

Whether or not a student reached that final stage in the program, we knew that each person at the center would nonetheless represent an entire family changed. For each disabled person participating, there would be one less parent having to choose between feeding his entire family and attending to the needs of one. There would be one less parent burdened by the guilt of leaving an immobile child, one less child who lay at home, abandoned and afraid. There would be one less disabled person reduced to begging, one less human edged out by society. Perhaps begging could be eliminated entirely as new opportunities reduced its labor force to none. Yet most importantly, the cloud of disdain that had settled on the disabled would be lifted, a forgotten blight on the history of society.

We didn't limit ourselves to the boundaries of the programs, however. When it came time to staff the center, we sought out disabled people to fill those roles, as well. Not only would this provide our students with empathetic teachers who understood their struggles more than anyone, it would also be employing yet another disabled Rwandan. Eventually, we would find an expert tailor to teach our sewing classes. Because of a leg deformity, he required forearm crutches to walk, but few could beat his skill and talent on a sewing machine. A blind woman would come to teach students how to operate our donated knitting machine. And of course, there's me, the man with no hands lending a hand to the disabled.

Throughout the planning process, as Zacharie and I mapped out our path to respectfully assisting the disabled, one idea was solidified in our minds and throughout the programs: disability is *not* inability. That was our driving truth. And we were out to prove that truth to the world.

In February 2008, construction on the center officially began. It seemed that the whole town of Gisenyi had come out to build our dream, from laying the foundation to nailing on the roof. It never occurred to me that our finished project would not only help the disabled, but in the meantime also provide months of work for everyone else.

As the building began to take form, it grew larger and more stunning than even I had imagined. There was an office with enough room for two desks and filing cabinets and even a couple of chairs. A storeroom and a smaller room sat off to one side, and the other side connected to our Learning Center, complete with several computer workstations. There was a classroom for the mentally challenged, and one for deaf children, separated by a partition from an equally large classroom where adult classes and other general activities would be held. Another building housed our adult crafting center, with a sewing machine workspace, tables for the banana-leaf crafting, and floor-to-ceiling shelves to store and display the handmade crafts.

Well before they rolled on that last coat of yellow paint, I could hear children laughing in the courtyard, see the deaf signing in the classroom, feel the coarseness of woven banana-leaf crafts the adults had made. It was all too good to be true. And yet, there it was—all of my hopes realized, an oasis for the outcasts of Gisenyi.

Finally, in November 2008, the Ubumwe Community Center was unveiled in a dedication ceremony open to all of Gisenyi. It was well attended by both current and prospective students, Jack and Suzi Hanna, supporters from the Columbus Zoo and PIC, Jessica McCall, and even a representative from President Paul Kagame's office. Jack kicked off the celebration with the dedication, and the rest of the day was a dreamy blur and evidence of all that could happen when people had enough faith to step out and build a dream.

thirteen

people like me

> *"Although the world is full of suffering, it is full also of the overcoming of it."*
> —HELEN KELLER

I can honestly say that I'm as enamored by the UCC today as I was on its opening day in November 2008, maybe even more so. Countless lives have been changed within the walls of this center—and beyond—but none more than my own.

One of the most defining moments for me was when my mother first visited the center. I had told her about it before, but I don't think she realized the scale of what we were doing until she saw it for herself. It was as if seeing the center and all of the people we were helping reconciled so many things for her. She told me then that she was sorry for ever implying that it would have been better for me to die and my sister to live. While we had each come to terms with the death of Mukamana, she knew, as I did, that God had spared my life for the good of all these people.

Now, not only have we seen each of our programs through

to a reality, but we've also added other program developments. Some of them have been relatively minor. We've added jewelry making to our work skills program, crafting colorful papier-mâché beads from recycled calendars donated by the Columbus Zoo and having our jewelry makers design necklaces, earrings, and bracelets from those beads. We have also, with the support of PIC, begun to provide prosthetics for some of our students and adults and have created a prosthetic repair and maintenance station onsite. We're able to serve a hot meal to everyone at the center each day, supported in part by the large garden we've planted behind the center that provides the vegetables we add to the meals.

Buying land with room to grow proved a wise investment when, in 2011, we broke ground on our Inzu Y'Abana (House of Children) preschool, located behind the main building of the UCC. Early in 2013, through the continued support of Congregation B'nai B'rith in Santa Barbara, California, the preschool opened as yet another means of integrating our disabled students with mainstream children. As with the other programs in the UCC, our focus would be on disabled children. But unlike the other programs, the preschool would be open to mainstream students: both children of those who work in and attend the center, as well as the entire community. The disabled students, as well as the children of people within the center, would be given priority and would attend at no cost. Mainstream students from throughout the community would pay a typical private preschool tuition. To further ensure that our preschool would rival any other in the area, we sought out the best teachers from other preschools and offered to pay them more to teach in our new school.

The preschool allows our students and our community to begin the process of integration at an even earlier age. And with the mainstream students in the minority, they would come to recognize a disability as a common condition, as simply another unique characteristic of their dearest friends. We know that these experiences can change generations as they carry those attitudes of acceptance into their adult lives.

As if the preschool opening weren't progress enough, we were also offered funding to build a primary school and began construction that same year. Thanks to the enthusiastic support of a family in Ohio, our preschool students will have a primary school to attend when they're ready to move up. As with the preschool, there will be tuition for mainstream students, and for disabled students we're starting a child sponsorship program. This will allow us to enroll even more disabled students by covering the individual expenses—books, supplies, uniforms—along with a portion of the operating expenses for the school itself. But for our disabled students, the addition of a primary school means that all children, disabled alongside mainstream, will have access to a complete basic education, equal to that of the mainstream students throughout our community. In the meantime, while we are awaiting the completion of our two-story school building, we have already begun the year-one primary classes in the conference room at the preschool. We are so fervent in this effort to educate our students, because deep down we know that education is the only path to sustained peace.

Even more amazing to me than the construction of new buildings and the development of new programs is the building and development of the people themselves, these people like me. It seems that at least weekly there is another moving story of lives being changed and hope being restored as a result of this center.

There was one baby boy who was born with a physical deformity. His parents had decided to abandon him in the trash, but as they wrapped him in a blanket and laid him in a box, the baby looked up at them and smiled. That smile awakened his parents to their ability to love a disabled child, but even then, they didn't know how to care for him. When they heard about the UCC, they came to us for guidance, and through counseling, the UCC is helping those parents to care for their disabled son.

Some children walk to the center from as far as the Congo to attend school every day. There's one seven-year-old big sister who walks her little five-year-old brother across the border to the center before making her own way to primary school alone.

Then there are those like Paul, locked away in their homes for years before the UCC services were available. Paul has a mental disability, and like many other parents of disabled children, his locked the door to keep him safe inside when they went out to farm. For twenty-five years, the only world Paul knew, the only experiences he had, were there within the confines of his home. But now Paul spends his days at the UCC. He's free to roam the fenced-in property, enjoying the sports and sunshine, he socializes with others like him, and he is learning skills that he can one day put to use supporting himself.

Pascar spent his days much as Paul did, wasting away at home in an isolated, rural area with his family. He was one of the first to find his way to the UCC, and after he showed his talents in sewing and paper crafting, we brought him on as a teacher. Now, Pascar not only is guiding and mentoring other disabled students, but is also a husband and father to two children of his own.

At the age of ten, one student survived an illness but was left blind as a result, forcing her to relearn her world without the advantage of sight. The UCC illuminated that world, showing her how to make banana-leaf crafts and even how to use the knitting machine. She now encourages others to come to the center, telling them that they are useful and able despite their difference in abilities.

Those who have left the center continue to inspire me with all they've accomplished. With funding from PIC, we've recently added an artisan association to our Moving into Action program, assisting the graduates who have gone on to use their skills in sewing, doll-making, banana-leaf design, or weaving. The association supports their transition into independence and their efforts by renting work space, providing sewing machines, and planting other seeds that will help their businesses grow.

Marie, now in her twenties, came to the UCC about three years ago. She had lived with her parents who, unlike most, were able to afford tuition to a program for people with disabilities, one of the few now in existence. But because of the deformity in her leg that left her struggling to walk, she wasn't able to find a job. That's when she heard about the UCC. After a year here, practicing banana crafting, sewing, using the knitting machine, and learning computer skills, she has started her own business, supported in part by our artisan association.

At one time, I—along with most everyone else in this area—bought into the assumption that the only means of survival for the disabled was a meaningless life of street-side begging. But through the UCC, I've proven myself and everyone else wrong in that assumption. By facilitating a program that propels the disabled into their full potential, they now are taking on the respected roles of business owners.

Probably the biggest factor of our success is the assurance of support from our selfless sponsors who have made our passions their own. PIC continues to fund our annual operating expenses and always finds a way to cover the cost of new teachers as the need arises. Jessie's Place, Congregation B'nai B'rith, and their generous donors have stepped up each time we've dreamed up a new expansion. Without a doubt, this financial security affords Zacharie and me the time and energy to focus on the continued expansion and evolution of the program itself, which, truth be told, probably only results in new ideas that need to be funded!

However, our long-term goal is to be completely self-sustaining. So when we discovered a few natural extensions of the center that would offset some expenses, we seized the opportunity. While the center itself is open to students on weekdays, we've found a way to put the center to work on nights and weekends as well. A local church was happy to rent our classrooms for their Sunday services, and a teacher pays to use the classrooms on weeknights. We've also opened a boutique at the center to sell the items made by our students, giving the student 40 percent of the sale price.

The remaining 60 percent goes back to the center: 40 percent to cover the cost of materials and 20 percent saved for future repairs on the sewing and weaving machines.

We've gone from serving a handful of students in a single room to serving almost five hundred through our various programs, and that number is continually growing. We have students ranging in age from preschoolers all the way up to a couple of men and women who are completing their master's degrees through distance-learning courses. With each perfectly formed body that walks or rolls through our gates, we've proven that all people are capable of living fulfilling lives, even—or *especially*—if they are people like me.

If you ever visit our beautiful country, drive west until you see the shores of the glistening Lake Kivu. Although you'll likely be enticed by the aroma of grilled fish and fried potatoes rolling out of Mama Chakura's kitchen, you'll also be within a Rwandan's walking distance of the Ubumwe Community Center. As you make your way down the rusty, rutted road, the city kids will run and wave behind you, calling out, "Umuzungu! Umuzungu!" And when you stop to say hello, regardless of the time of day, they'll carefully articulate, "Good morning," through broad, beaming smiles. You'll step through the gate, connected to a fence that frames a lush, manicured lawn, and a bright-yellow building will reflect the hope of the Rwandan sun. It is then that you will know: you've reached your oasis.

You'll be lifted by the laughter of children playing ball. You'll be enchanted by the deaf school girls chatting on the wooden benches. You will no doubt stop to watch the blind men cutting strips of dried banana leaf and weaving them into placemats and potholders, developing skills that will one day feed their families.

And there will be dancing. Yes, before you can refuse, you'll be drawn in to the clapping, singing, and dancing that welcome you home. It's our way of saying, "Come, see all that is beautiful here. See it, and rejoice."

It is my hope that, here at Ubumwe, you will be awed by the differences you find. The blind men lead the way. The deaf teach you to speak. And the fingerless teach you to feel. But above all, you will be welcome here; you will be one of us. Because when you think about it, we are *all* people like me.

fourteen
i am able

"Disability is not inability."
—Ubumwe Community Center

A couple of years ago, I was back at Charlene's house, relaxing after the dizzying bustle of the Rwandan Fête, an annual fund-raiser for PIC held at the Columbus Zoo. Charlene's husband, Bob, asked, "So, Frederick, what's next? What are you going to do this next year?"

By this time, they knew the way my mind worked. They knew I was always looking forward, always thinking of the next thing to build on the foundations that had already been laid. I want to show the world—really, the *entire world*—that even if you have disabilities, you are able to do anything. And I was always planning new ways to reach that goal.

"I'm going to do a bicycling campaign."

Bob was the first to respond. "*What?!* How are you going to do that?"

Charlene smiled, sharing his sentiment. Yet they both already knew that I would find a way to make it happen. For me, from the moment I had the idea, I knew that it wasn't just an idea. It was more of a vision—I saw myself doing it. I had no doubt that it could be done—that it *would* be done.

Christy, their daughter, grabbed a pad of paper and a pen. "This is huge," she said, shaking her head and scratching out notes on the paper as we talked.

I told them that I had noticed, over the years, how interested people were every time they would see me riding my bicycle and even a motorcycle. I wanted to use that opportunity, that natural interest, as a way to create more awareness about disabilities. I explained how I wanted to do a cross-country bike ride, stopping in the villages and marketplaces to show how a "disabled" man could ride his bike with no hands.

They all pitched in with ideas, suggesting people to contact and thinking through the logistics of an extended bike ride. We talked about dates and locations. And together, we came up with the name: I Am Able. It would not only serve as the campaign name, but also as our simple, driving mantra.

When I returned to Rwanda a few weeks later, I immediately began training, riding the steep, curvy roads of Rwanda. I had been riding a bike with no hands for years. And I've also been known to raise a few eyebrows at the motorcycle track when I rev and ride the motos you can rent there, just as any two-handed man would dare to ride. But I knew that this would be completely different. I knew a bicycle campaign would require stamina and strength, nothing like my short bicycle trips around town.

I learned a long time ago that it's better not to use my fingers while I'm riding because my skin provides a better grip and feel of the tension in the handlebars. The riding itself felt completely natural, but with each ride, I tried to push myself to ride a little faster and a little farther.

As I practiced, I was always met with the enthusiasm of inquisitive kids. They waved to me and ran along beside me as I rode. And when I stopped, the brave ones would ask me what I was doing, riding a bike with no hands. Others stood to the side, eyeing me curiously. I would always answer and explain, shaking their hands and allowing them to see that my skin, my arms, were really just like theirs.

For my first official ride, I planned a daylong trip, circling through several villages and towns within a fifteen to twenty-kilometer radius. I provided the local radio station with my schedule, so that local villagers would know where and when they could see me pass through. We did a call-in portion of the radio show, and it seemed everyone wanted to know the same thing: "How are you going to make it? How are you going to do this without help?"

As other people like me heard about my journey, as they watched me practice and prepare, some of them asked if they could join me. One of the first was an American woman, Christie Abel. I had first met Christie at the Imbabazi Orphanage a few years ago and later saw her in California. When she heard about the ride, she immediately began looking for sponsors, created a brochure, and offered to take photos along the ride. Then came Innocent Twagirumukiza, who at first glance doesn't appear to have any handicap, but an old gunshot wound had greatly diminished the strength and maneuverability of one of his arms. And Innocent Mugabo had polio in one leg, leaving one leg weaker and shorter than the other. Dositha's right hand was cut off after the genocide when she was a baby, and Safari had lost one of his legs while fighting for the army.

When each of them asked to join, I answered, "I don't know. Are you able?"

Without fail, they would answer, "Yes. I am able."

And with each answer, our project grew.

While the rest of my team was willing, most of them didn't have their own bicycles, and few of them had bicycles appropriate for a daylong ride. But with Christie's help, we raised enough money to rent bicycles for everyone. Charlene's daughter, Christy, raised funds for food and to hire a car to follow us in case anyone needed a rest or needed to ride the rest of the way home.

A longtime friend, Ziri, also offered to come along to help. I first met Ziri when I had just left the Imbabazi and was living in my own place. He was about seven years old and living on the streets. I learned that his parents had been killed around the same time that I had lost my hands. I just couldn't leave him out on the streets alone, so I brought him home to stay with me. Over the years, I saw to it that he went to school, and he helped me around the house. Now he's an independent adult, working for a tourism company, giving bicycle tours and helping people with their luggage. Ziri was a much-needed member of our bicycling team. He was well acquainted with bicycling the Rwandan hills. Plus, he could pull another bicycle alongside him as he rode in case someone got tired and needed to rest in the car for a while.

Finally, it felt like everything was in place.

The morning of the ride, the excitement coursed through our group. Smiles were wide; legs were pumping. We followed the winding roads of Gisenyi-town to Ryabizige, stopping at small villages along the way to rest. At Ryabizige, a huge crowd of probably five hundred people had gathered to see us. As a group, we tried to speak to all of them, to answer the questions, to demonstrate how a man with no hands or a weak leg can ride a bicycle.

The questions were endless. They wanted to know how I even learned to ride a bike in the first place.

"Well," I answered, "I just never gave up. I wanted to do it for myself, but I also wanted to show people that I am able to ride without hands."

As the questions kept coming, the people watched in wonder as our little group—one that would typically be rendered useless beggars in society—set an example of relentless ability, breaking down the paradigms that ostracized the disabled.

From Ryabizige, we went to Rwerere up to Mudende back through Rubavu down to Kanama up to the village Pfunda and back to Gisenyi, stopping to visit wherever there was a small crowd gathered. The Imbabazi, which was along our route, had offered to provide lunch for us, so we stopped in and had a wonderful lunch with the staff. They had prepared bread and honey, oranges, small bananas, rice and vegetables, and tea and milk. It was the perfect place to find refreshment for our long ride home.

When we returned to the center, where we had started from early that morning, a crowd had gathered to welcome us home. They were cheering and laughing, amazed that we had even returned at all. We were blissfully exhausted. We had shown the world—well, at least our little corner of it—that we were, in fact, able.

"How did you make it?" someone asked.

A burst of energy returned. I hopped up on my bike and rode circles on the driveway.

"Easy! See?" I laughed, holding my head high, gliding and maneuvering the handlebars with natural ease.

The crowd burst into laughter and the cheering erupted again.

When the group finally dissipated and our team members said their good-byes, I couldn't help but feel satisfied. Our goal was to change the way people looked at disabilities, as well as their own abilities. We wanted to show parents that their disabled children had different abilities, to show disabled children and adults that disabilities didn't render them useless. We wanted to show *everyone* that anything is truly possible if you try.

And I believe that, in some small way, we did.

Before I fell asleep that night, I had already begun planning the next phase, to take our project a little further, to build it a little bigger. I want to take I Am Able to villages we've never been to, to people who haven't heard our story, who've never seen a disabled person bicycling through town. My dream is to take a bigger team around the entire country—even around the world. I already have plans to visit Ohio, Colorado, and California, and will be talking soon with someone in England about the program too.

So, if you're in those areas, watch out! Join in!

I want everyone to hear and see I Am Able. I want them to know that they are able.

We *all* are able.

fifteen

rebuilding hope

"You do not teach the paths of the forest to an old gorilla. Rather, watch him and learn."
—AFRICAN PROVERB

Inspired by both the leadership of our president and the lowliness of beggars, we Rwandans are all doing our part to rebuild hope in a country so ravaged by hate. International media has taken note of our progress, of how far we've come in such a short time. Much of that is owed to the incorruptible, innovative leadership we've had in place over the last couple of decades. However, such leadership would have had little impact on a people any less resilient and responsive than Rwandans. We welcomed the rigid reform that went as far as restricting the use of plastic bags in an effort to keep our country clean. We wanted our country to initiate immediate change; we knew all too well the cost of allowing anything less.

In our little corner of Rwanda, Zacharie and I are a single example of that resilience and response. We've set out to show our fellow citizens that a handicap is not a punishment from God; it is simply another challenge to overcome. To that end, we hold an annual celebration to exhibit the beauty of disability. It's an all-day event where people come from all over to dance and show their awareness and acceptance of people like me. The I Am Able campaign will help to carry the spirit of that day throughout the year, and I hope, eventually, throughout the world.

As for my painting endeavors, technically, I guess you could say that I'm now a professional. I've found my niche in creating oil and acrylic landscapes that try to capture the breathtaking beauty of Rwanda and her people: hills set against an African sky or basket-topped silhouettes of women walking beneath the banana trees. I first began selling my paintings at the Columbus Zoo in Ohio, and now PIC sells them every year in the African marketplace at the Rwandan Fête. I've done demonstrations in schools along with my speeches, just to inspire the children— fully abled children—not to be limited by their circumstances, to put no limits on what they perceive as possible. People never seem to tire of witnessing landscapes come to life from an artist with no hands. And I never seem to tire of painting them.

And that house I wanted to build? Well, that has partially come true. I bought a home in Gisenyi, which is now a town of about ten thousand people. The house is like several others along the street there, with a couple of divided storefronts at the street and the living quarters in the back. As with most modern homes in town, it has electricity but does not yet have running water. And I'm just a short walk from getting Internet at a café. For now, I am living in one of the storefronts until the construction is finished on the expansion in the back. Each time I save enough money, I complete another phase of the construction—the walls, the roof. In the meantime, I'm renting out the other storefront to a business owner as another means of making an income. So yes, while I do have a home of my own, I've decided, at least for now, that I'd rather hire someone else to climb the roof and hammer the nails.

As for the UCC, our vision is to have centers in every corner of our country, where people with different disabilities can meet to socialize and to share their challenges, supporting one another in unity. We're always brainstorming new ideas for expanding and improving the center, like adding a one-room medical clinic and a music therapy room. Rwandan officials have even expressed an interest in using the UCC as a model for others like it across the country. Like so many other Rwandans initiating change, we didn't set out to be revolutionary. We just set out to do what was right.

Although Madame Rosamond Carr died in 2006 at the age of ninety-four, the Imbabazi is still carrying on her legacy of nurturing the children of Rwanda. During a recent visit back to the Imbabazi Orphanage, I learned that because of the government's nationwide initiative to place every orphan within a family, the Imbabazi was transitioning out of its role as an orphanage. In support of the government's initiative, the orphanage launched the Reunification Project to find homes for its remaining children through relatives or close family friends. Once all of the children had been placed, the Imbabazi continued to provide financial aid for those families to ensure that the child's education and quality of life was maintained. The Imbabazi has also recently announced that it will be transitioning into the role of a preschool, a still-rare opportunity for the youngest generations of Rwandans.

As for beggars, you don't see many of them anymore. The government is working to get them off the streets by sending them to school and teaching them trades that they can use to support themselves. By getting them off the streets and into self-supporting jobs, it not only raises the morale of an individual; it also works to raise the morale of a country.

There are countless other efforts being made by countless other individuals across our country. On the last Saturday of each month, businesses shut down for a few hours in the morning for Umuganda, meaning "community service." At that time, the whole nation—the president included—comes out to clean the streets of Rwanda. People everywhere can be seen sweeping the streets or picking up trash as a whole, and the result, as anyone who's been to Rwanda will tell you, is that it's one of the cleanest countries in the world. Much of this, I think, is due to our people all coming together to build a country that everyone can take pride in.

High in the Virunga Mountains, there are guides who double as guards for our endangered mountain gorillas and their habitat. Many of those guides and other employees in the Virunga National Park were once poachers who now protect the very animals they were paid to hunt. But when the park made it more profitable and reliable to protect the animals, these poachers made the change that was ultimately for the good of all.

Every June, animal lovers from around the world flock to Rwanda to celebrate the survival of these gorillas at Kwita Izina, our annual gorilla-naming ceremony. This international celebration commemorates the birth of new gorillas by giving each of them official names and announcing them to the world. The endangered mountain gorillas that make their home in the Virunga Mountains are one of our most precious resources, and as a country we're coming together to celebrate that, raising conservation awareness while focusing on a positive aspect that sets our country apart from the rest of the world.

For me, those majestic, enduring creatures remind me of how far I've come. Although these living, breathing wonders of the world were only a few hours away from my home, I had never been to see them. Any time I would mention the desire to go, I was always politely told that I couldn't make the hike through the dense mountainous forest. It was strongly suggested that you'd have to use a walking stick to make the hike, and, well, I obviously couldn't hold one.

As of this writing, I have now completed the hike to see the mountain gorillas five different times. I've been with Jack Hanna, tourists, friends, and students. From that very first hike, I realized that while the trek could be strenuous, it was nowhere near as difficult as it had been portrayed to me. I found that I was able to hike as well as anyone, even without a walking stick—or hands, for that matter. While everyone else seemed to require the extra assistance, I just didn't need it.

To show his support for our country, Jack Hanna has gone as far as to build a house here, right at the foot of the mountain gorillas' home. In doing so, he hopes to show the world that Rwanda has grown so far past the horrors of the genocide; he meets regularly with President Kagame and advocates Rwanda as one of the cleanest, safest countries he's ever visited. In appearances around the world, he beckons people to come and explore Rwanda—the culture, the landscape, the gorillas—and all of the treasures of our country for themselves.

One large motivator of our national progress is President Kagame's Vision 2020, a plan to lift Rwandan citizens out of poverty and into an educated middle class. It was set into motion in 2000. Then, in 2001, a new flag, national symbols, and national anthem were revealed. The anthem, "Rwanda Nziza," meaning "Beautiful Rwanda," captures the spirit of all-encompassing peace and unity not only in its lyrics, but also in its origins. The song's lyrics were written by a prisoner, while the music was composed by a member of the Rwandan Army Brass Band. Throughout Kagame's presidency, he has proven that he wants Rwandans as citizens, as well as Rwanda as a nation, to become self-sufficient and a model for the African world.

Now the progress of his Vision 2020 can be seen all over the country. As you walk through our capital city of Kigali, you'll see new housing developments springing up that would fit right into any bustling American metropolis. Old high-rises are being demolished and replaced with state-of-the-art construction. Even in the smaller villages, old homes that no longer meet the basic codes requirements are being marked for demolition. In fact, when I recently went back to visit Claudine, the younger of the sisters who saved me the night my hands were cut off, we went by her old home where I had spent that night. On the front of the home was a large X, indicating that the empty house would soon be torn down.

April 7 of every year is a day that reminds all Rwandans of how far we've come. The day marks the start of an entire week dedicated to remembering the genocide. Citizens across our country spend the week in quiet remembrance of loved ones they lost and in somber reflection of how such racial hatred was allowed to develop.

Those mass killings rocked my childhood and forever changed my life; they forever changed the lives of most every Rwandan. But now, enough time has passed that the children of Rwanda will have no personal experience of such atrocities. While they may still be affected by the social and economic aftermath of the event, this generation will have a childhood full of progress and hope.

When you visit our country today, there is little evidence that such vitriolic hate ever existed here. From the bustling city of Kigali to the rural hills of Ramba, the people are happy and hopeful. The most evident reminder of the genocide and its aftermath are the memorials intentionally erected throughout the countryside. The largest of these is in Kigali, built on the site where more than 250,000 genocide victims are buried. As you walk through the somber hallways, backlit panels tell the story behind those horrific one hundred days and the history that generated the genocide, the darkest days in our history, when a million Rwandans were senselessly slain. The second level of the memorial expands the view to the all-too-numerous genocides that have occurred throughout the history of the world.

These memorials serve as a reminder to us all—they're a call to reflect on the damage caused when we allow hate to flourish. By being reminded of and resistant to that hate, we can be assured that we will never again allow the evil of discrimination and exclusion to creep into our countries, into our lives. And in doing so, we can again be open to the full capacity for hope.

epilogue
boundless hope

During my first trip to the United States in 2003, after I got my fingers, I presented my story to the public for the first time, thanking the PIC supporters for all they had done to support the orphanage and my trip. There were about six hundred people in the audience that night, all staring at me as I spoke in very broken English. I received much prompting and translation from Charlene as I spoke, but in the end, the attentive audience took away the message of hope and forgiveness just the same. After the event, it seemed as if all six hundred of them came and thanked me, wanted to hug me, and wanted to hear more.

Since then, I've gradually improved as I've spoken to thousands of people, from coast to coast, through a variety of media. I've spoken in Ohio numerous times, almost annually at the Rwandan Fête, updating our supporters on the progress at the UCC. I've spoken to groups in New York, Florida, and California, delivered a TEDx Talk, done newspaper interviews, and now written a book. My English still is not perfect, but no matter how I deliver the message, the feedback is always the same: people everywhere struggle with forgiveness, and everyone is hungry for hope.

When you get down to it, I think we all have our handicaps. Of course, for a guy with no hands, my handicap is a little more obvious. And by wearing my handicap on the outside, I've learned how to speak about the trauma and the struggles that go along with it.

People are more likely to show compassion to me, or a lady in a wheelchair, or a blind man using a cane to feel his way around. But what about those with hidden handicaps? How do we address those with unspoken fears and broken hearts, undelivered apologies and never-noticed hurts, faded bruises but memories that never will?

Disability of the spirit is so much more debilitating than a physical disability. Yet we tend to be less sensitive to those hidden handicaps. But these are the broken ones who seem to most identify with me as I speak to audiences around the country.

One man approached me after a speech at the Fête and asked me how I was able to forgive someone who had caused such trauma to me. I explained how forgiveness was like applying the medicine of peace to your heart. Another woman from California hadn't been able to forgive her sister after a trip together had gone terribly wrong. But something within my speech helped her to see the importance of forgiveness.

Through it all, one thing has become clear: we are all broken. We all must learn to forgive and live again. The alternative is unacceptable. And the challenge, the trial, the pain only serves to make us stronger.

The good thing is this: although we all are broken, we all have the same offer to be made whole again. We all have a God who wants to lift us up from our dusty, dirty brokenness and piece us back together again, making us something more beautiful than when we began and perhaps even leaving a few cracks so that His glory can shine through.

———✶———

Many years ago, my life was spared at the market by the serendipitous intervention of Hamatha, a blind business owner. At the time, blinded by fear myself, the magnitude of that moment never even registered. But looking back now, God's mysterious ways become so perfectly clear. As early as that first time He spared me, He was calling to me, setting my entire life's purpose in motion. When I reached that lowest point of despair, when I thought there was no other way, He had already shown it to me through that disabled, independent man—if only I'd had the faith to see.

Through that God-given desire to help people like me, I hope to have set a ripple in motion, one that will stir into a tsunami and in some way help to wash away the evil that ravaged our country those many years ago, the evil that ravages us all. In the same way that God used Hamatha to spare my life and show me the way, I hope He uses me as that same protective, guiding light for others.

But more than anything, I pray that everyone will listen to the gentle nudge of His whisper: "Look, child, *this* is what is possible when you have boundless hope."

acknowledgments

From Frederick

First and most important, I give sincere thanks to the Lord God for allowing the completion of our work and for protecting me throughout the many obstacles during my life. Without Him, there would be no story; my story is His, and all of its glory goes to Him.

I would to like to thank my mum, Anne Marie Nyirakobwa, and my family who have supported and guided me during my life and taught me the importance of working hard, working together, and never giving up.

A special thanks to Rosamond Carr in heaven for caring for me after I lost my hands, also to Charlene and Bobby Jendry, Jeff Ramsey, and Jack and Suzi Hanna for being my ambassadors to the United States and for making it possible for me to have hands once again. And thank you to the Columbus Zoo, Partners In Conservation, Jessie's Place, Congregation B'nai

B'rith, the Ellen Hunter family, John Seigel, Terri Kepes, and all of our individual sponsors for your continued support of the Ubumwe Community Center. You have all been an integral part of helping me overcome my adversities and fulfill my dreams.

Zacharie Dusingizimana, from my English teacher at the Imbabazi Orphanage many years ago to my business partner today, you have been by my side through it all, contributing your love and patience to care for "people like me."

Words cannot express my deep appreciation to Amy Parker, who helped to organize this book, and to all who helped me throughout this book.

I cannot conclude this list without a thought to my colleagues and friends at the Ubumwe Community Center. You inspire me to keep going every day.

From Amy

My dear friend, Frederick Ndabaramiye, you have changed my life. You have inspired me, opened my eyes, and shushed my excuses. I'm not sure how to thank someone for a gift like that, but I know that these words are not enough.

Daniel Parker, my wisest counsel, IT guy, accountant, accountability partner, travel buddy, compass reader, videographer, editor, problem solver, manager, defender, and Prince Charming, I hope you know that I would not, could not do any of this without you, and I'll spend the rest of my life thanking you for that. I love you infinitely.

And to my two favorite boys, Michael and Ethan, thank you for traveling with me, understanding when we traveled without you, taking notes, eating frozen pizzas, and just being quiet while Mom was working. You bring me joy that you will never fully comprehend—I hope you know how much I love you.

Jack Hanna, I feel like a broken record. Thank you, thank you, thank you for introducing me to Frederick, for introducing me to Rwanda, for putting your name and enthusiasm behind this book. Thank-yous will never be enough. I am eternally indebted.

To my parents—Mom and Gary, Daddy and Sherry, Mr. and Mrs. Parker—you are not only the reason I say, "I can do it." You are the reason I believe it. I am so grateful for you all.

To Laura Smith, Requelle Raley, Toni Birdsong, Jamie Chavez, and my entire creative support group—you know who you are, and you fuel every word, every late night, every success. May chocolate and coffee and pure creative bliss follow you all the days of your lives.

And to the Author of this story and all of our stories, thank You for this latest chapter in mine. Your ability to work through an incompetent slug like me amazes me daily. Your grace gets me through. This is all Yours.

From Frederick and Amy

This book is the definition of team effort. There are so many different fingerprints all over these pages and so many people without whom this book really, truly would not have been possible.

Zacharie Dusingizimana, you have been so gracious with your time and so generous with your knowledge on this project.

You are such a huge part of this story. We hope it makes you proud.

Jack Hanna, Kate Oliphint, Erin Ensign, Charlene Jendry, we know how much you and your teams have poured into this story; there is no way to measure the depth and width and height of our gratitude.

Many thanks to John Kulewicz, Jason Elvers, and the team at Vorys for your willingness to answer legal questions ad nauseam. Bill Reeves, Brian Mitchell, and the Working Title Agency, you've juggled all of the balls of this project with the skill and charisma of a circus clown. We thank you.

Adria Haley, Andrea Lucado, Caroline Green, Darcie Clemen, Emily Sweeney, Kristi Smith, Matt Baugher, and the entire HCCP team, thank you for capturing the vision and for loving this project as much as we do. It has made all the difference.

Thank you, all of you, for believing wholeheartedly in this idea and for putting your whole hearts behind it.

about the authors

Frederick Ndabaramiye is a Rwandan who lived through the genocide and its aftermath. He is cofounder of the Ubumwe Community Center, an organization that helps "people like me" to discover their purpose and abilities in spite of their circumstances. After losing his hands in post-genocide conflicts, Frederick lived in the Imbabazi Orphanage, where he met Zacharie Dusingizimana. Together they founded and operate a community center, preschool, and primary school that serve the people of Gisenyi, Rwanda, and the surrounding areas. Frederick frequently visits the United States, speaking annually at the Rwandan Fête at the Columbus Zoo and other various speaking engagements all over the country, including a TEDx Talk in Columbus. He is also a gifted painter who can often be found riding his bicycle on the streets of Gisenyi and beyond.

You can find Frederick and his I Am Able page on Facebook and learn more about the UCC at UbumweCenter.org.

Amy Parker is a best-selling author of more than twenty books, with well over a half million copies sold. She loves to collaborate with other best-selling authors—such as Jack Hanna, Andy Andrews, and Michael Catt—in telling their stories too. Two of these collaborations—*Firebird* and *Courageous Teens*—are recipients of Christian Retailing's Best Awards. But Amy's greatest reward is being a wife to Daniel and a mom to their amazing sons, Michael and Ethan.

Visit Amy Parker on Facebook, Twitter (@amyparker), and at AmyParkerBooks.com.